Chez Panisse
Pasta, Pizza, & Calzone

The Chez Panisse Cookbook Library

Chez Panisse Cooking
Chez Panisse Desserts
Chez Panisse Menu Cookbook
Chez Panisse Pasta, Pizza, & Calzone

CHEZ PANISSE

PASTA PIZZA & CALZONE

BY
ALICE WATERS
PATRICIA CURTAN
&
MARTINE LABRO

RANDOM HOUSE
NEW YORK

Illustrations by Martine Labro
Book Design by Patricia Curtan

Copyright © 1984 by Tango Rose, Inc.

All rights reserved under International and Pan-American Copyright Conventions.
Published in the United States by Random House, Inc., New York,
and simultaneously in Canada by Random House of Canada Limited, Toronto.

This work was originally published in hardcover by Random House, Inc., in 1984.

Library of Congress Cataloging-in-Publication Data

Waters, Alice.
Chez Panisse pasta, pizza, & calzone.

Includes index.
1. Cookery (Macaroni)   2. Pizza.   3. Calzone.   4. Chez Panisse.
I. Curtan, Patricia.   II. Labro, Martine.   III. Title.   IV. Title: Chez Panisse
pasta, pizza, and calzone.
TX809.M17W35   1984   641.8   83-43186
Hardcover Edition ISBN 0-394-53094-2
Paperback Edition ISBN 0-679-75536-5

Manufactured in the United States of America on acid-free paper

Paperback Edition Printing
9 8 7 6

Hardcover Edition Printing
9 8

This book is dedicated to our children
Fanny, Zachary, and Camille.

Acknowledgments

We wish to thank our tasters and family, Stephen Thomas, Stephen Singer, John Hudspeth, and Claude and Camille Labro. We are very grateful for the technical advice and expertise of Fritz Streiff, Will Powers, Elaine Ginger, Janet Kessel, and David Goines. Special thanks and appreciation to those suppliers and producers of wonderful foodstuffs: Paul Johnson and the Monterey Fish staff, Kathleen and Robert Stewart, the Chino Ranch, Karen Lake, the Cheeseboard, Green Gulch Zen Center Farm, and the Acme Bread Company. We especially want to thank Jason Epstein, our editor at Random House, for his great good faith and confidence, which allowed us the freedom of spirit to create and design this book exactly the way we wanted.

Contents

SUMMER PASTA

FALL PASTA

WINTER PASTA

PIZZA

THE PASTA

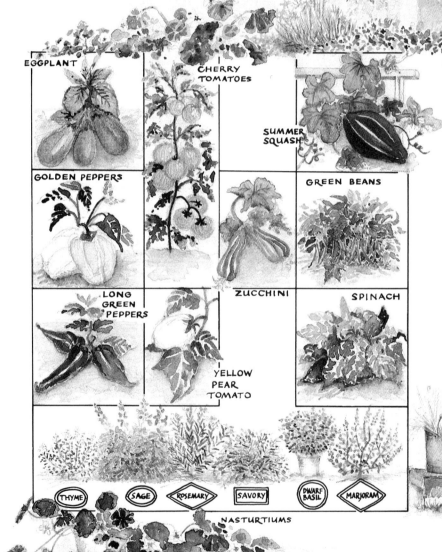

EGGPLANT

CHERRY TOMATOES

SUMMER SQUASH

GOLDEN PEPPERS

GREEN BEANS

LONG GREEN PEPPERS

ZUCCHINI

SPINACH

YELLOW PEAR TOMATO

THYME   SAGE   ROSEMARY   SAVORY   DWARF BASIL   MARJORAM

NASTURTIUMS

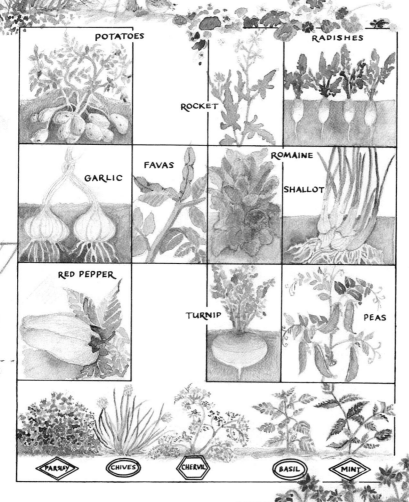

GARDEN

POTATOES

RADISHES

ROCKET

GARLIC

FAVAS

ROMAINE

SHALLOT

RED PEPPER

TURNIP

PEAS

PARSLEY

CHIVES

CHERVIL

BASIL

MINT

BORAGE

Martine Labro

Introduction

Why pasta and pizza? To begin with, Chez Panisse has always had strong Mediterranean affinities. We share the same climate and many of the same raw materials. The down-to-earth, lighthearted cuisines of Provence and Italy are a constant source of inspiration – grilled radicchio and anchovies, roasted peppers and garlic, brandade, crusty pizzas baked in wood-burning ovens, mussels and fennel, saffron and tomato fish stews. This is informal food with lively direct flavors. But this cookbook is not a regional, historical, or encylopedic treatment of the subject. It's meant as an introduction to our style of pasta and pizza: more Provençal than Italian in inspiration, highly personal in execution.

The pasta recipes appear in a seasonal format to show how naturally cooking can reflect the time of year and the kinds of ingredients you might find in a modest kitchen garden. Where pasta is concerned, we generally prefer fresh homemade pasta – thin, delicate, and soft. Pasta is extremely satisfying to make not only because it's cheap and easy, but because very delicate fresh pasta simply can't be bought. Our recipes reflect our prejudice for hand processing. Handmade pasta is great to eat and to look at when it has pleasant irregularities: slightly uneven hand-cut noodles look beautiful and taste better, too, because they cook slightly unevenly, resulting in agreeable differences in texture. You can use little metal dies and get absolutely identical, uniform ravioli, but we prefer the looks of larger hand-cut ravioli, with no two exactly alike.

There are also recipes here for dried pasta in a number of different machine-made shapes; our goal has been to match certain sauces and ingredients with the right type and shape of pasta, and for certain dishes – some salads, for example – dried pasta works best.

Pizza has the same immediate appeal as pasta, and it satisfies in the same way. The same principles apply to making it: use a light hand (avoid too much cheese!) and avoid overcomplicated combinations of ingredients. Many of the same combinations of flavors work with both pasta and pizza. Above all, feel free to experiment with many different combinations and variations. Like pasta dough, pizza dough can be flavored in different ways. Try incorporating herbs into the dough – or anchovies or dried tomatoes.

Most of the recipes in this book were directly inspired by the harvest of a small kitchen garden. The picture of our "pasta" garden will give you some idea of the possibilities. If you plant a garden it can change your entire style of cooking. Even a tiny plot with just a few herbs, some salad greens, garlic, leeks, and beans can have a dramatic effect. So much commercial produce is grown for its looks and keeping properties, not for flavor, and there is so much standardization of mass-produced food that we are in danger of forgetting how much variety there can be. Refrigeration, freezing, and packaging technology make it possible for us to eat nothing but the same bland, processed flavors year round. But a small-scale garden can open up a new world of grateful subservience to the seasons. Gardening can become your primary source of culinary inspiration: to be able to go to your back yard, pick something, and make a wonderful, simple, impromptu dish of pasta with it is immensely gratifying. Of course, not everyone can have a garden; but you can befriend people who do, and even some commercial truck farmers and market gardeners attempt to meet the demand for produce grown for quality, not yield.

Our hope is to inspire you rather than direct you. You really need only some conception of the possibilities and a little curiosity. Be receptive to variety and improvisation. We've given you some practical pasta and pizza survival techniques along the way, but our main intent is to share our enthusiasm and whimsy.

Chez Panisse
Pasta, Pizza, & Calzone

Flours & Doughs

All-purpose white flour in this country is generally a blend of hard and soft varieties of wheat. Hard and soft refers to the relative gluten content of the wheat, the substance that allows the dough to form a strong and elastic structure. Almost all brands are "enriched" with vitamins and minerals to approximate those contained in the wheat germ, which is not present in white flour. Those labeled "bleached" have been chemically bleached to a uniform whiteness which the manufacturers believe makes a more salable product. This unnecessary process removes some of the flavor and character from the flour.

Whole-wheat flour is milled from the entire wheat berry which includes the wheat germ (with its vitamins, minerals, proteins, and oils) and bran, the fibrous layer surrounding the germ and wheat berry.

Semolina flour is made from very hard or high-gluten wheat, usually durum wheat, which is a hard yellow variety. Generally not ground as fine as our white flours, it has a slightly granular texture. Because of its high gluten content, it makes a strong, fast-drying pasta most suitable for commercial production.

Buckwheat is not a variety of wheat at all, but a weed related to rhubarb. The plant produces bunches of white flowers, the seeds of which are ground to make buckwheat flour. It is nutritious and very flavorful, but since it contains no gluten, it must be blended with wheat flour to make any sort of dough.

Very different pasta doughs can be made from these flours, singly or in combination. The basic dough, made with all-purpose flour and rolled very thin, is fine textured, very delicate, and light. It is particularly well suited to cream sauces, and makes excellent ravioli and lasagne. Pasta made with a combination of white flour and whole-wheat flour has a nutty, breadlike flavor and an interesting texture, because of the fiber content of the bran and wheat germ in the whole grain. Dough made with semolina and white flour has a toothy resilient character that is great when made into slightly thick linguine, and for pasta dishes requiring a noodle with real body. Buckwheat pasta is tender and earthy with a deep, maltlike flavor; it is beautiful in short, wide, hand-cut strips that suit its peasant flavor.

The quality of the flour is an important consideration in making good pasta, but what is often overlooked is the quality of the eggs. The difference between a dough made with a regular market egg and one

5

from a homegrown chicken is dramatic. Chickens that are well fed and allowed to run and scratch, and not fed steroids and antibiotics, produce remarkable eggs. The yolks are intensely yellow and flavorful, and the texture, especially of the whites, is firm and gelatinous and quite unlike the weak, watery, mass-produced egg. They make golden, silky, tasty noodles. Seek out the best source you can find for fresh, real eggs. They will make an incredible difference in your pasta.

The pasta doughs in these recipes were made by hand and rolled with a hand-cranked pasta machine: the kind that clamps onto a work surface, has adjustable settings for the rollers, and various cutting attachments. Rolling the dough is very straightforward, but there are some tricks that are helpful in problem situations.

First, use your hands to mold the dough to an evenly flat, rectangular shape that will be easy for the machine to accept. Put it through the various settings and avoid flouring the dough. If it is properly firm — that is, not too moist — it won't require flour. If it is a little soft, use a minimum of flour and cut the dough into shorter lengths about midway through the rolling. These are easier to control than one long piece that will fold over on itself and stick together. To prevent the pasta from folding over on itself at the sides as it goes through the rollers, use your free hand to hold the strip of dough back a little and provide tension.

Individual machines vary quite a bit at the last setting, number 6 or 7, depending on the type. Some will roll the pasta too thin and even tear it at that setting, and yet at the next-to-the-last setting, the dough may not be quite as thin as you want it. A solution is to roll the pasta several times through the next-to-last setting, which will make the dough a little thinner each time through, until it has the desired thickness. This also applies to a machine whose final setting does not roll the pasta thin enough. Keep putting the dough through until it is the way you want it.

When you have rolled the pasta to the desired thickness, flour it lightly before putting it through the cutter. This will prevent the pasta from sticking together as it comes out of the cutter, and when you cut the lengths with a knife. Short lengths are much more manageable than long ones, especially when mixing the pasta with the sauce and other ingredients, and they make attractive servings on the plate. Toss the cut noodles well to separate them, let them air dry a few minutes on the table, and then refrigerate. They will stay soft and fresh in the refrigerator several hours before beginning to dry.

The shapes and cuts of pasta called for in the recipes have been determined largely by the standard cutting attachments available with most hand-cranked pasta machines. Tagliatelle is the wider noodle, about ¼ inch wide. Taglierini is the narrow noodle, about ¹⁄₁₆ inch wide. Spaghetti is made using the narrow cutter with a thicker sheet of pasta, rolled to setting number 4 or 5. Fettuccine is hand cut, a little wider than tagliatelle, and about ⅜ inch wide. Linguine, cut by hand or with a cutting attachment available with some machines, is about ⅛ inch wide. Pappardelle hand cut with a knife or zig-zag wheel cutter is about 1 inch wide. In all cases unless otherwise specified we mean fresh pasta rolled thin.

We suggest two methods of cutting the pasta by hand. Flour the sheet of pasta, cut into the desired length of noodle, loosely roll the sheet into a cylinder, and cut through with a knife at even intervals. Then toss with your fingers to loosen and separate the pasta. Or lay the sheet of pasta out flat in front of you, flour it lightly, and use a knife or wheel cutter to cut the pasta crosswise to the desired width. This will result in noodles that are as long as the width of the sheet of pasta. This works very well for fettuccine and pappardelle.

Both fresh and dried pasta should be cooked in a large pot of rapidly boiling salted water, at least 4 to 6 quarts. Fresh pasta cooks very fast. Very thin noodles, rolled to setting number 5 or 6 on a hand-cranked pasta machine, will cook in 30 to 60 seconds. Slightly thicker noodles will cook in 1½ to 2 minutes. Dried pasta takes considerably longer, usually 6 to 8 minutes, depending on the type of noodle; check the directions on the package. Taste for doneness. The cooked pasta should not taste raw and doughy. It should be firm and a little resilient. If overcooked, the pasta will be soggy, weak, and tasteless.

An excellent tool for removing the pasta from the boiling water is a large Chinese wire-mesh spoon, the sort that is broad and shallow with an open wire construction and a long bamboo handle. They are inexpensive and always available in Chinese markets. Scoop up the pasta with the spoon, let the water drain away, and put it directly into the pan with the sauce and other ingredients or on a warm serving dish. We find this method simpler and faster than pouring the entire contents of the pot into a colander.

Another indispensable tool is a pair of V-shaped metal tongs. They should be strong and lightweight with a piece of spring steel at the base. The tongs make it possible to toss and serve the pasta easily with one hand, leaving the other free to hold the pan or dish.

Basic Pasta Dough

Proportions

    1 cup unbleached all-purpose flour
    A little salt
    1 egg
    A little water, if necessary

Start with good quality flour. Put it in a bowl with the salt and make a well in the center. Add the beaten egg, and working with the finger-tips, begin to blend flour and egg from the center out, gradually gathering the flour from the sides. Mix the flour and the egg, getting the particles next to each other without actually working or kneading the dough. When you have the flour and egg mixed, add a few drops of water and begin to bring it all together as a mass. Turn it out onto a table and begin to knead. It will take several minutes to produce a very firm, smooth, and strong dough. The amount of moisture in the dough is the most critical element: this varies according to the size of the egg and type of flour. As the dough comes together, decide whether a little water is needed, or whether it is too soft and requires a little more flour. Do this at the beginning, because the dough will resist the addition of flour or water after you really begin working it. It is better if the dough is on the dry side, making it necessary to add a few sprinklings of water as you knead, than to try to incorporate more flour into dough that is too soft. When you have the right amount of moisture in the dough – and experience will teach you what that is – knead the paste for 10 to 15 minutes, then cover it to prevent a dry skin from forming and let it rest at least 45 minutes before rolling and cutting.

Green Pasta

6 to 8 ounces fresh spinach leaves
Optional: ½ cup Italian parsley leaves
2 cups all-purpose flour
1 egg
Salt

9

De-stem, wash, and dry the spinach leaves. (The addition of Italian parsley will give the pasta real flavor.) Purée the raw leaves as smooth as possible in a food processor or blender; you should have ⅓ cup dense purée. Mix the beaten egg, purée, and salt. Proceed as in the basic dough recipe.

Whole-Wheat Pasta

½ cup whole-wheat flour
½ cup all-purpose flour
1 egg
Salt
Water

Semolina Pasta

½ cup semolina flour
½ cup all-purpose flour
1 egg
Salt
2 teaspoons or more water

Buckwheat Pasta

⅓ cup buckwheat flour
⅔ cup all-purpose flour
Salt
1 egg
1 to 2 teaspoons water

The method for making the pastas with different flours is the same as the basic pasta dough recipe. The harder flours with more gluten will require more water.

It is nearly impossible to make pasta by hand with all semolina flour; the flour is too hard and resistant to moisture. Commercially, it is made by machines and never really forms a cohesive dough but is a rather dry granular mass that is extruded under great pressure through brass dies.

Herb Pasta

There are many variations possible with different kinds and quantities of herbs. A green pasta can be made with all kinds of green leaves: parsley, sorrel, rocket, marjoram, hyssop, borage, basil, and so on. Or the pasta can be flavored with a single herb such as sage or rosemary – 2 teaspoons of the finely minced herb per basic 1-egg recipe.

Black Pepper Pasta
Add 1 tablespoon freshly ground coarse black pepper per 1-egg recipe.

Red Pepper Pasta
Add 1 teaspoon crushed red pepper per basic 1-egg recipe.

Saffron Pasta
Soak a pinch of saffron threads in 1 teaspoon hot water. Add the water to the egg and proceed as usual.

A note on portions
The recipes do not call for exact quantities of pasta. This is rather a matter of personal discretion, whether you and your family or guests are big eaters, and whether you serve the pasta as a first course, a main course, or as an accompaniment to something else. Generally speaking, a 1-egg, 1-cup-of-flour pasta recipe will make 2 large servings, 3 medium servings, or 4 small hors d'oeuvre-size servings. The important ratio is the relative amount of pasta to the other ingredients. We prefer nearly equal proportions of pasta to the other ingredients in the recipes. The recipes are designed for moderate-sized portions.

11

Lasagne Technique

We cannot overemphasize the importance of rolling the pasta for lasagne as thin as possible. Everyone has had lasagne made from those thick dry noodles with curled edges, usually layered with too much rubbery bland cheese, and a sauce made from canned tomatoes and handfuls of dried "Italian" herbs. In great contrast, lasagne can be made with very thin light noodles, layered with a creamy pesto sauce, the whole wrapped like a package in pasta and baked so that it gently steams and puffs, with just the top becoming crispy and brown.

Roll the pasta very thin. Cut the sheet of dough in lengths to fit your dish – actually, a little smaller, because the pasta will expand when it cooks. Let the pasta dry for 15 to 20 minutes. Have ready a pot of salted boiling water and a bowl of cold water. Don't cook all of your pasta at one time but just enough for one or two layers. Cook the pasta, 2 or 3 sheets at a time, for 30 to 40 seconds. Lift them from the boiling water and immediately submerge them in cold water. Lift from the cold water and spread out flat on a towel to absorb the water. Careful handling is required once the pasta is dry, as it will stick together if it folds back on itself. At this point the pasta is ready to be layered in the dish with the sauce and whatever else the lasagne is to contain.

An interesting way to construct the lasagne is to make the first layer with sheets of dough covering the bottom of the dish and continuing over the sides. Layer the sauce and pasta until the dish is full, then fold those first sheets of dough up over the top, as if wrapping a package. This seals in the sauce and the flavors while the lasagne cooks.

Ravioli Technique

It is worthwhile to be well organized before beginning to make your ravioli. Consider the textures of different fillings. Some things such as artichoke hearts and potatoes with garlic are well suited to a smooth purée, while fine hand chopping is the best for other ingredients, such as shellfish or wild mushrooms. As a general rule, the ravioli filling should not be too wet. Too much moisture will make the dough on the bottom soggy and sticky. If the stuffing is quite moist, you will need to cook the ravioli soon after forming them. Most fillings will do quite well for a couple of hours in the refrigerator. Have the filling cold or at room temperature. Do not roll too much dough at one time or the sheets will begin to dry and be difficult to work with by the time you get to them.

Roll the pasta dough to the thinnest setting of the machine. Do not

12

use flour during the rolling unless absolutely necessary. At the end of the rolling, lightly flour the sheets of pasta cut into lengths 12 to 18 inches long. Working on a lightly floured table, take one section at a time and fold it in half lengthwise. Unfold it and use the center crease as a guideline for placement of the filling. Put a teaspoon or more of filling every 2 inches, just under the center line of the bottom half of the strip of pasta. Spray the pasta with a fine mist of water or use a pastry brush to lightly moisten the dough around the filling. Fold the top half of the dough over the filling and bottom half of the dough and press firmly between and around the mounds of filling. Take care to avoid air pockets. Lightly flour the strip of ravioli and use a cutter-crimper to cut off the uneven bottom edge the length of the strip. Then cut in between the pockets of filling to form the individual ravioli. This cutter-crimper device effectively cuts the dough and seals the ravioli in one motion, whereas a zig-zag wheel only cuts the dough. Set the ravioli on a floured baking sheet so they don't touch, and refrigerate until they are ready to be cooked.

Cappelletti Technique

Roll the pasta dough very thin. Cut manageable lengths of dough, 12 to 18 inches long. Cut one sheet at a time into approximately 2-by-2-inch squares with either a plain wheel cutter or one with a zig-zag edge. Place ½ to 1 teaspoon of filling in the center of the square. Moisten the edges of the dough with water, using your fingertip or a pastry brush. Fold the dough in half into a triangular shape over the filling, and press the edges firmly together. Wrap the triangle around your finger and press two points together to form the little stuffed pastas that are supposed to resemble bishop's hats.

Tortellini Technique

Tortellini are made in a similar fashion. Use a cookie cutter to cut circles of dough 1½ to 2 inches in diameter. Place ½ teaspoon or so of filling in the center, moisten the edges, and fold the dough over to form a half moon. Wrap the half moon around your finger and press the ends together firmly.

13

Cook ravioli, cappelletti, tortellini, and the like in a large pot of gently boiling salted water. If the water is boiling vigorously it can cause some of the ravioli, etc., to open. Cook stuffed pastas made from very thin dough approximately 3 minutes. If the dough is a little thicker, simmer for 4 to 5 minutes. A good way to cook ravioli, tortellini, and so on to be served in broth or sauce is to half cook them in boiling salted water, lift them from the water, and let them finish cooking in the simmering broth or sauce. This allows more flavor to penetrate the dough and stuffing.

It is our profound desire that this book inspire you to invent your own pasta dishes and pizza with whatever ingredients you happen to have. Some of the recipes are very specific because we know the techniques or particular combinations and proportions of ingredients will produce delicious results. Other recipes are purposely vague because the *exact* quantities or methods are not important. Few dishes ever come out the same way twice: it is rare that exactly the same ingredients are ever assembled again, and different cooks cooking the same recipe will usually achieve very different results. We hope you will use this book as a source of suggestions and feel free to take an idea from one recipe and a technique from another and make up your own recipe to suit your mood, or craving, or timing, or whatever. The variations found at the end of some recipes are intended to be used in this spirit.

SPRING
PASTA

Martine Lebre

In the spring the skies clear, the mood lifts, and palates hunger for something new and alive after winter's diet of slow-cooked, stored-up foods: tender new shoots or wild green things, like stream sorrel and miner's lettuce; the first morels; the first little radishes and garden greens. . . . I think of foods that remind me of birth and renewal: little animals like spring lamb and suckling pig; quail eggs and salmon roe; fiddleheads and wild asparagus. Springtime seems to call for more subtle and delicate combinations of flavors to accompany pasta. Garlic is used, but less frequently, and in its immature green form. Young fava beans and sweet green peas appear on menus again and again.

The best spring menus sound fresh and lively: salmon roe, peas, and linguine; poached salmon; and Meyer lemon sherbet. Or pasta with white asparagus, brown butter, and Parmesan; a mixed grill of quail, liver, and sausage; and tangerine sherbet. For a special spring feast this year at the restaurant we grilled the first local salmon and followed it with green garlic ravioli, baby lamb, a salad with nasturtiums, and finally ice cream scented with plum blossoms. Less lavish, but still springlike, another dinner might begin with pasta with fava beans, saffron, and crème fraîche; have as its second course a plate of steamed mussels; and end with a puff pastry tart with the very first *fraises des bois*.

I remember a particularly savory lunch at Martine's house: pasta with grilled artichokes, pancetta, and thyme, and cheese and fruit for dessert. (Artichokes are often very good in the spring, and many cheeses are at their best, too.) Ideas for simple meals with just a salad and a pasta dish are easy to think up: imagine pasta with crab, peas, and olive oil, followed by a salad of little red and green oak leaf lettuces; or a miner's lettuce salad followed by pasta with fresh morels and garden carrots.

Springtime wines that go with these menus range from the very light, slightly sparkling Italian Prosecco to fine Burgundies and California Pinot Noirs. One thing to look for in the spring is good California white wines. Many wineries release their Chenin Blanc, Gewürztraminer, and Sauvignon Blanc in the spring; some of these will be best drunk soon after, with dishes like pasta with tiny shrimp, peas, and crème fraîche.

WHITE ASPARAGUS, BROWN BUTTER, PARMESAN, & FETTUCCINE

1½ pounds white asparagus
½ cup sweet butter
Fettuccine for 4
Salt and pepper
Parmesan

Serves 4

PEEL THE ASPARAGUS and brown the butter. Heat the butter gently until it begins to turn golden brown and has the strong aroma of toasted nuts, then stop the cooking. Cook the asparagus in boiling salted water until tender but not limp, approximately 5 to 6 minutes. Drain and add to the pan with the warm butter. Cook the thin noodles and toss them in the butter. Season with salt and pepper. Serve the noodles with the asparagus all around and a young moist Parmesan shaved over the top.

Variations: Sliced white truffles could be an additional garnish for this pasta. – Substitute fiddleheads or wild asparagus for the white asparagus.

ASPARAGUS & ARTICHOKE HEART PASTA

1½ pounds asparagus
4 large globe artichokes
Juice of 1 lemon
4 shallots
A handful fresh basil leaves
2 to 3 tablespoons sweet butter
1½ cups chicken stock
1 cup heavy cream
1 tablespoon Pommery or Dijon mustard
Salt and pepper
Tagliatelle for 4

Serves 4

CUT THE TIPS from the asparagus stalks and wash them well to remove any sand or grit. If they are large, cut into halves or quarters lengthwise. Save the stalks to make soup or purée, or for some other use. Remove all the outer leaves of the artichokes and pare down to the heart. Trim away the green leaf ends, the choke, and the stem. Cut the heart into 8 wedges, and leave them in water with the lemon juice until ready to cook. Peel and thinly slice the shallots. Cut the basil into ribbons.

MELT THE SHALLOTS in a few tablespoons of butter. Add the chicken stock, gently reduce to about a cup, then add the cream. Meanwhile, blanch the artichokes in boiling salted water 4 to 5 minutes until tender, then add to the sauce. Blanch the asparagus. When the tips are tender (2 to 3 minutes for thin asparagus, 5 to 6 minutes for fat asparagus), add them to the sauce. Add the mustard and basil and taste for salt and pepper. If the sauce is too thin, reduce it a little more. Cook the pasta and add to the pan. Toss in the cream sauce and serve garnished with the vegetables.

Variations: A versatile sauce with the artichokes and asparagus is the mustard herb butter on page 130 – Fry chicken hearts in a little butter and olive oil with shallots, then combine with the artichoke hearts and mustard sauce.

22

GRILLED ARTICHOKES,
PANCETTA, THYME, & TAGLIATELLE

2 pounds tiny artichokes
8 tablespoons virgin olive oil
Salt and pepper
⅓ pound pancetta, sliced
A large bunch fresh thyme
Tagliatelle for 4

Serves 4

TRIM THE ARTICHOKES of the outer leaves, leaving just the pale, tender inner leaves and the heart. Cut them in half and marinate in 5 tablespoons olive oil for an hour. Season the artichokes with salt and pepper and grill them over a charcoal fire until browned and tender. When cool, cut the halves again into quarters. Cut the pancetta slices into lardoons and brown gently. Stem a large handful of thyme leaves.

FRY THE PANCETTA, thyme, and artichokes together in the remaining olive oil and pancetta fat until thoroughly hot. Cook the pasta and add to the artichokes. Toss everything together and serve. These grilled artichokes are really delicious and by themselves make a great hors d'oeuvre.

23

FETTUCCINE, WILD MUSHROOMS, & PROSCIUTTO

¼ pound sugar snap peas
4 slices prosciutto
2 cloves garlic
½ onion
Several sprigs fresh parsley
⅓ to ½ pound *Lepiota rhacodes* mushrooms
2 to 3 tablespoons virgin olive oil
Salt and pepper
½ cup chicken stock
Fettuccine for 2

Serves 2

LEPIOTA MUSHROOMS, commonly called "shaggy parasols," have a strong meaty flavor. The taste is lively and aggressive, very different from the delicate morel. The flavor is best brought out by frying them hot so that they brown a little. They normally have a fair amount of forest dirt clinging to the stalk and cap which can be removed with either a soft mushroom brush, a cloth, or a small knife to cut away the really stubborn parts, such as the base of the stalk. A combination of these techniques will work well. When clean, cut them into thin slices. Once cut and exposed to the air, the flesh will turn a light apricot color. They have a long season in California, from the first rains in the fall to the last in the late spring.

Wash and string the sugar peas, and cut them in half lengthwise. Cut the prosciutto slices into small strips. Peel and chop the garlic. Peel and dice the onion. Chop the parsley fine.

SAUTÉ THE MUSHROOMS in hot olive oil. Add the onion and season with salt and pepper. After a few minutes, lower the heat and add the garlic and the peas. Cook another minute or two and add the prosciutto and chicken stock. Cook the pasta and add to the mushrooms. Toss all together, taste for seasoning, and serve garnished with parsley and more black pepper.

Variations: Wild mushrooms, a single variety or a combination of species, are delicious with pasta just by themselves. Slice the mushrooms and fry them in a combination of butter and olive oil. Add some chopped parsley and garlic, salt and pepper, and toss with the noodles. Chanterelles are very good with an addition of cream. Shaved white truffles make an excellent garnish. – Grill whole chanterelles over a charcoal fire, then put them in a roasting pan and moisten with some good stock. Cover the pan and bake in the oven or over the charcoal fire until tender. Cut them into smaller pieces or slices. Reheat them in the stock and add some butter. Spoon the mushrooms and sauce over pasta tossed in butter with salt and pepper and garnish with chopped parsley.

25

FRESH MORELS, GARDEN CARROTS, & LINGUINE

½ pound fresh morels
3 shallots
8 or 10 baby carrots
Several sprigs each
 fresh chervil and thyme
Several sprigs fresh parsley

2 to 3 tablespoons sweet butter
Salt and pepper
½ cup reduced chicken stock
¾ cup heavy cream
Lemon juice
Linguine for 4

Serves 4

FRESH WILD MUSHROOMS should not be washed. Morels are usually very clean but should they have a little dirt, use a brush or cloth to gently clean them. Slice the mushrooms thin. Peel and dice the shallots. Peel the small carrots and cut them into a fine julienne. Pluck the leaves of the chervil and thyme and finely chop them together. Finely chop the parsley.

SAUTÉ THE MUSHROOMS and shallots in butter for a few minutes. Add the carrots, chervil, and thyme and season with salt and pepper. Sauté another minute or two then add the stock and cream. Let the sauce gently reduce by about a third, but do not allow it to become too thick. By this time the carrots will be cooked tender and the cream will be infused with the delicate mushroom flavor. Taste for salt and pepper. A squeeze of lemon juice will bring up all the flavors. Cook the pasta and mix into the cream with the vegetables. Serve garnished with chopped parsley.

Variations: Chanterelles, blewits, shaggy parasols, and so on, can be used instead of morels. – A mirepoix of onions, celery, artichoke hearts, fennel, or shallots can replace the garden carrots. – If you have a little black truffle, it will be used to advantage if soaked in the cream to flavor the sauce.

FETTUCCINE, FAVA BEANS, SAFFRON, & CRÈME FRAÎCHE

½ pound fava beans
1 tablespoon virgin olive oil
1 clove garlic, chopped
Salt and pepper
A few fresh basil leaves
¾ cup crème fraîche
Saffron
Fettuccine for 2
Fresh chives

Serves 2

SHELL AND SKIN the fava beans (see page 177). Cook them gently in olive oil with the chopped garlic for 2 to 3 minutes. Season with salt and pepper. Add some basil leaves cut in ribbons, the crème fraîche, and a small pinch of saffron. Cook another few minutes, then cook the fettuccine and add to the beans. Season the noodles with salt and pepper and toss with the favas. Serve garnished with a sprinkling of chives.

Variation: Sauté small squash blossoms, 4 or 5 per person, in olive oil with chopped green onion. Add blanched green beans and a pinch of saffron. Cook and add fettuccine, season with salt and pepper, and serve garnished with some of the green onion stalk cut very fine.

TAGLIATELLE, FAVA BEANS, PANCETTA, & CHICKEN

1 chicken breast
A handful fresh basil leaves
6 to 8 tablespoons virgin olive oil
10 very thin slices pancetta
2 stalks celery
2 cloves garlic
1 cup fava beans
Salt and pepper
Tagliatelle for 2
Parmesan

Serves 2

BONE THE CHICKEN breast and remove the skin and fat. Cut chicken crosswise into very thin even slices. Cut the basil leaves into narrow ribbons and marinate with the chicken in a little of the olive oil. Unroll the pancetta slices and cut them into small sections. Wash the celery stalks and slice thin. Peel and finely chop the garlic. Shell the fava beans and peel them (see page 177).

IN A SMALL PAN, fry the pancetta until crisp and light brown. Sauté the chicken in 3 or 4 tablespoons olive oil that is hot enough to sear the meat in the first 20 or 30 seconds. Season with salt and pepper, then add the celery, fava beans, and garlic and reduce to medium heat. Cook for another minute or two, stirring frequently. Add the pancetta and 3 or 4 more tablespoons olive oil. Cook the noodles and toss with the meat and vegetables. Serve garnished with more ground black pepper and freshly grated Parmesan.

Variation: Add or substitute other green vegetables: asparagus, peas, leeks, and so on.

FENNEL, CRAB, CHERVIL, & LINGUINE

1 bulb fennel
A handful fresh parsley leaves
A few bay leaves
1 lemon, sliced
Salt and pepper
2 Dungeness crabs,
  preferably live
2 carrots

2 shallots
2 stalks celery
6 green onions
A small bunch fresh chervil
2 to 3 tablespoons sweet butter
1½ cups heavy cream
Linguine for 6

Serves 6

PUT A LARGE POT of water on the stove to boil. Season it with fennel tops cut from the bulb, parsley stems, a few bay leaves, lemon slices, and enough salt to approximate sea water. When it reaches a rolling boil, drop in the live crabs and cook for 6 or 7 minutes. Take the crabs from the water and let them cool.

Make a mirepoix by finely dicing the carrots, shallots, celery, fennel (use only the tender center if the outside layer is tough), and green onions (use only the white part and save the green stalks for garnish). Finely chop the parsley and chervil.

Clean the crabs. Crack the shells and remove the meat (see page 177).

SAUTÉ THE MIREPOIX in a few tablespoons butter until tender but still a little crunchy. Add the cream, herbs, and crab meat. Season with salt and pepper and lemon juice. Cook the thin linguine and add to the pan. Mix well and serve garnished with the green onion stalks, cut very fine.

Variation: Blend crème fraîche and lemon zest to taste. Heat the cream and add shelled crab meat. Serve over hot noodles garnished with chives and pepper.

30

CRAB, PEAS, OLIVE OIL, & SPAGHETTI

Salt and pepper
A few fresh parsley stems
A few lemon slices
1 bay leaf
One 2½ to 3 pound Dungeness crab, preferably live
A handful fresh basil leaves
3 green onions
1½ cups shelled peas
5 to 6 tablespoons virgin olive oil
Spaghetti for 3

Serves 3

HEAT A LARGE POT of water to boiling. Season it with salt, parsley stems, lemon, and bay leaf. Slip the live crab into the water and boil for 6 or 7 minutes. Remove from the water and let it cool. Cut the basil leaves into narrow ribbons. Cut the green onions into a julienne. Clean the crab, crack the shells, and remove the meat (see page 177).

GENTLY COOK the peas in olive oil for 2 to 3 minutes. Season with salt and pepper and add the crab meat and basil. Cook the spaghetti and add to the pan, along with the green onions. Toss all together, taste for seasoning, and serve.

Variations: Make a sauce with a combination of olive oil and crème fraîche, instead of just olive oil. – Cook the crab and shell the meat. Sauté thinly sliced fennel bulb in olive oil. At the last minute add the crab meat and a little chopped fennel top and season with lemon juice, black pepper, a few drops of Pernod, and toss with the pasta. – Or boil the live crab 2 minutes. Remove, break into parts, and finish cooking on the grill over a charcoal fire. Shell the meat. Grill some hot smoked sausage and cut in slices. Sauté red onion in olive oil, add some peeled and seeded tomato, and then the sausage and crab. Toss with pasta and garnish with fresh green onion.

PASTA WITH PEAS, SPINACH, & PROSCIUTTO

⅓ pound sugar snap peas
2 bunches spinach
2 or 3 cloves garlic
8 slices prosciutto
6 tablespoons sweet butter
3 to 4 tablespoons virgin olive oil
Salt and pepper
Tagliatelle for 4

Serves 4

WASH THE PEAS well, then snap off each end and pull the string down the side. Cut each pea pod in half lengthwise. Selectively edit the spinach leaves. Peel and finely chop the garlic. Cut the slices of prosciutto into small pieces.

MELT 4 TABLESPOONS butter and olive oil in the pan and gently sauté the peas for a minute or so. Season with salt and pepper and add the garlic. Begin to add the spinach by handfuls. As the leaves wilt, add another handful until all are wilted. Add the prosciutto and let everything stew together a few minutes. Cook the pasta and add to the pan with another 2 tablespoons butter. Toss all together. Season with additional ground black pepper and serve.

Variation: Add or substitute other green vegetables: fava beans, green beans, asparagus, whole young shallots or onions, or chard and other greens.

GARDEN PEAS, CRÈME FRAÎCHE, & TAGLIERINI

1 pound peas
1 bunch watercress
2 tablespoons virgin olive oil
1 handful fresh basil leaves
6 tablespoons crème fraîche
Taglierini for 2

Serves 2

FRESH PEAS are essential for the success of this pasta dish. They should be small, juicy, and sweet. The more commonly available pea that is large, dry, starchy – and sometimes even starting to sprout – simply will not do.

Shell the peas. You should have approximately 1 cup. Wash and dry the watercress and remove the leaves from the stems and cut into narrow ribbons.

GENTLY COOK the peas in the olive oil for 2 to 3 minutes. Add the watercress, basil, and crème fraîche and cook a few minutes more. Cook the taglierini and add to the peas. Season with salt and pepper. Mix all together and serve.

SALMON ROE, PEAS, & LINGUINE

1½ pounds sugar snap peas
2 to 3 tablespoons virgin olive oil
1 cup crème fraîche
Salt and pepper
Linguine for 4
8 to 10 ounces salmon caviar
Fresh chives

Serves 4

THE MOST IMPORTANT ingredient in this dish is the peas. Sugar snap peas have edible pods. The ones you find in the market will vary as to size and maturity. The younger peas are less developed and less sweet inside, but the pods are quite delectable. The older peas have pods that are rather tired and tough, but the peas inside are sweet. A nice way to deal with them is to eat the whole pea, pod and all, of the younger ones, and shell the older ones, saving just the peas. For this recipe choose a third of the best-looking pods and shell the rest. Pull the strings from the pea pods and cut them lengthwise in three.

SAUTÉ THE PODS in the olive oil very gently for 4 to 5 minutes. Add the crème fraîche and shelled peas, and season with salt and pepper. Let this simmer the minute or so it takes to boil the linguine. Drain the pasta, then add to the peas and toss together. Remove from the fire, add the salmon caviar, and toss gently once more. The caviar and the shelled peas have nearly the same texture and will pop between your tongue and palate. Garnish with a sprinkling of minced chives.

SHRIMP, PEAS, CRÈME FRAÎCHE, & SPAGHETTI

1¾ pounds whole shrimp
2 cloves garlic
A handful fresh basil leaves
3 to 4 tablespoons virgin olive oil
Salt and pepper
2 cups shelled fresh peas
¾ cup crème fraîche
Spaghetti for 4

Serves 4

WASH THE SHRIMP in cold water, remove the heads and peel off the shells. Peel and finely chop the garlic. Cut the basil leaves into narrow ribbons.

SAUTÉ THE SHRIMP in hot olive oil. Season with salt and pepper. After a minute, lower the heat and add the garlic and peas. Cook for 1 minute. Add the crème fraîche and basil and cook another minute or so. Cook the pasta and add to the pan. Mix well and taste for seasoning. Serve garnished with a little more fresh basil.

Variation: Other tender green vegetables or a combination of them such as asparagus, young shallots, baby leeks, spinach, green onions, fava beans, and so on, can be substituted for the peas.

FETTUCCINE WITH BROKEN GARLIC & PEAS

3 small heads fresh garlic
2 slices bacon
8 to 10 sage leaves
A small bunch fresh Italian parsley
½ pound sugar snap peas
1 tablespoon virgin olive oil
⅓ cup chicken stock
Fettuccine for 2
Salt and pepper

Serves 2

SEPARATE THE CLOVES of garlic. Use the side of a chef's knife or a cleaver to gently flatten the cloves. Slip off the skins. Cut the bacon in small cubes. Tear the sage leaves in 2 or 3 pieces and leave the parsley branches whole. Shell the peas.

FRY VERY GENTLY the garlic cloves, bacon, parsley, and sage in the olive oil. Very careful attention is necessary to keep the garlic from burning; stir constantly the 10 to 15 minutes it will take the garlic to become golden. Add the chicken stock and peas. Cook the pasta and add to the peas and garlic and toss all together. Season with salt and pepper and serve.

Variation: Another version of this dish can be made with dried pasta, lots of broken garlic, olive oil, salt and pepper, and garnished with deep-fried parsley branches.

37

FRIED VEAL, PEAS, & PAPPARDELLE

½ pound boneless veal
Salt and pepper
All-purpose flour
2 or 3 cloves garlic
A handful fresh Italian parsley
4 tablespoons sweet butter
Zest and juice of 1 lemon
1½ pounds peas
3 tablespoons virgin olive oil
Pappardelle for 4

Serves 4

CHOOSE boneless, tender veal cut from the loin or leg. Trim off any tendons or tough tissue. Cut the meat in slices and pound as for scaloppine, then cut the slices into strips. Season with salt and pepper and toss lightly in flour. Finely chop the garlic and parsley and mix with the butter. Season the mixture with salt and pepper and a little zest of lemon. Shell the peas.

FRY THE VEAL in hot olive oil for about 1 minute. Lower the heat, add the peas, and sauté about 1 more minute until the veal is just cooked. Cook the pasta and add it to the veal and peas, along with the garlic butter. Toss everything together, season with a squeeze of lemon juice, and serve.

GREEN GARLIC RAVIOLI

12 young garlic plants
4 to 5 tablespoons sweet butter
2 or 3 small new potatoes
Salt and pepper
1-egg pasta dough
  yield: 30 to 35 two-inch ravioli
1 cup chicken stock

Serves 4

THE YOUNG GARLICS are approximately six months old. Planted in late fall, they are harvested in late spring. Mature garlic, widely available commercially, is usually nine months in the ground and is then harvested and dried. These young garlics have developed distinct cloves inside but have not yet begun to form the skin surrounding each clove. The central stalk is soft, green, and not woody. If cut through, across the cloves, the texture is uniform, crisp, and moist. The upper green stalk has a fresh, leeklike flavor and texture. The flavor is definitely garlic, sweetly pungent and aromatic, without the hot, sharp taste of mature garlic.

CUT THE GARLIC bulbs from the stalks and peel off the outer layer of skin. Cut off the roots and quarter or halve the garlic bulbs so that they are all about the same size. Use half of the stalks and trim them as you would a green onion. Remove the dried outer layer and cut them into small sections. Stew the bulbs and stalks gently in 2 to 3 tablespoons butter until they are tender and soft enough to purée. Boil the new potatoes and when the garlic is ready, purée them together. Season with salt and pepper.

Roll the pasta and fill the ravioli (page 12). Boil the ravioli. When cooked, remove them to a pan with the chicken stock and 2 tablespoons butter heated together. Serve moistened with the broth and garnish with additional black pepper.

39

CUCUMBER & CHICKEN CAPPELLETTI

2 chicken breasts
½ cucumber
1 stalk celery
2 green onions
2 shallots
2 chanterelles
3 tablespoons sweet butter

1 tablespoon fresh marjoram leaves
Salt and pepper
1-egg pasta dough
  yield: 40 to 45 cappelletti
1 quart chicken stock
Fresh chives or green onion

Serves 4

COMPLETELY TRIM the chicken breasts of all skin, sinew, and fat and mince very fine. Peel and seed the cucumber and finely chop it. Use a vegetable peeler to remove the strings from the celery. Mince the celery and green onions. Dice the shallots and chanterelles and sauté in butter until soft. Finely chop the marjoram leaves. Mix everything together and season with salt and pepper. Form the cappelletti (see page 13). Half-cook them about 2 minutes in gently boiling salted water. Remove the cappelletti to a pan with the hot stock and simmer gently until completely cooked. Serve in bowls with the broth, garnished with chives or green onion.

Variations: Use roasted, instead of raw, chicken for the filling. – For a pasta with similar flavors, cook strips of chicken breast and cucumber in butter with chopped chervil and parsley, and add crème fraîche flavored with pepper and a little juice and zest of lime. Serve with fettuccine.

SMOKED CHICKEN & PASTA SALAD

1 to 1½ pounds smoked young chicken
2 dozen radishes
2 Gravenstein or McIntosh apples
3 large handfuls rocket leaves
½ to ¾ cup virgin olive oil
Balsamic vinegar
Coarse mustard
Lemon juice
Salt and pepper
Tagliatelle for 4

Serves 4

BONE THE CHICKEN and shred the meat. Thinly slice the radishes. Quarter, peel, core, and thinly slice the apples. Remove any large stems from the rocket and cut the leaves in 2 or 3 sections. Keep everything chilled. Make a lively vinaigrette to taste with the virgin olive oil, balsamic vinegar, mustard, lemon juice, salt, and black pepper.

Cook the pasta, drain and toss in a large bowl with 4 to 5 tablespoons virgin olive oil, salt, and pepper. Let it cool. Just before serving, mix it with all the other ingredients and dress with the vinaigrette.

Variation: Substitute smoked duck, smoked trout, or smoked sturgeon for the chicken.

GREEN BEANS, TAPENADE, & LINGUINE

4 dozen Gaeta olives
⅓ cup light olive oil
1½ salt-packed anchovies
3 or 4 cloves small fresh garlic
Dash of Cognac
2 large handfuls tiny green beans
Linguine for 4

Serves 4

PIT THE OLIVES and purée them with the olive oil in a blender or food processor. Rinse and filet the anchovies, then pound them to a smooth paste in a mortar. Peel the garlic and pound it to a paste as well. Blend part of the anchovies and part of the garlic with the olives; add each by degrees, tasting as you go. Because the intense flavors of the ingredients are so variable, the mixture must be made by taste and not by amount. The idea is to balance the flavors so that no one element dominates the others. A dash of Cognac provides a sweetness and harmony to the sauce. Let the tapenade sit for an hour or so for the flavors to marry.

TOP AND TAIL the beans. Bring the pasta water to a boil and cook the beans about 2 minutes, until tender but still a little crunchy. Drain them, remove to a warm serving dish and toss with the tapenade. Boil the linguine and add to the beans. Toss again so that everything is well coated with the sauce and serve.

SPRING SHALLOTS, RED ONIONS, LEEKS, & PAPPARDELLE

10 or 12 each:
  Young shallots
  Small red onions
  Small yellow or white onions
  Baby leeks
  Whole heads young garlic
8 tablespoons sweet butter

Salt and pepper
Fresh thyme branches
2½ cups reduced
  squab or chicken stock
Pappardelle for 4
Fresh Italian parsley and chervil

Serves 4

TRIM ALL of the onions and garlic of their roots and uppermost stalks so that they remain whole with a few inches of green stalk. Sauté them in half of the butter for 5 to 8 minutes until they begin to brown. Season with salt, pepper, and a few thyme branches and add the warm bird stock. Simmer about 15 minutes until the vegetables are tender. Cook the pasta and toss it with the remaining butter and season with salt and pepper. Spoon the sauce and onions over the noodles and garnish with a few leaves of Italian parsley and chervil.

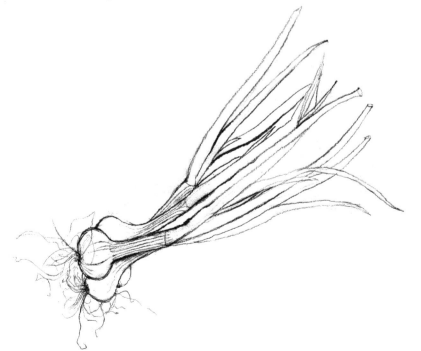

GARDEN SHALLOTS,
GRASS SHRIMP, & GREEN PASTA

½ pound tiny shrimp
4 young fresh shallots
½ cup fresh bread crumbs
5 to 6 tablespoons virgin olive oil
A small handful of rocket
Salt and pepper
¼ cup Provençal rosé wine
Green linguine for 2

Serves 2

RINSE THE SHRIMP in cold water and remove the heads and tails (see page 182). It is not necessary to remove the thin shells, which have a crunchy texture when fried. Finely chop the young shallots, including some of the green stalk. Fry the fresh bread crumbs in a little olive oil until they are golden. It is very easy to burn them, so they must be stirred constantly while cooking over a low flame. Cut the rocket leaves into thin ribbons.

FRY THE SHRIMP and shallots in a few tablespoons of olive oil. Season with salt and pepper. Cook over a high flame, stirring, for 2 to 3 minutes. Add the rosé wine and cook another 30 seconds. Cook the green linguine and add to the shrimp. Remove from the heat and add the bread crumbs and rocket. Toss all together, check the seasoning, and serve. The rosé is an excellent accompaniment.

Thyme Blossoms,
Oysters, & Green Fettuccine

12 oysters
2 shallots
Sprigs of flowering thyme
2 tablespoons sweet butter
Pepper
½ cup heavy cream
Lemon
Green fettuccine for 2

Serves 2

OPEN THE OYSTERS and save all of their juices. Peel the shallots and slice very thin. Pluck the little pink blossoms from the sprigs of flowering thyme, enough for a tablespoon of blossoms.

MELT THE BUTTER and gently sauté the shallots with a pinch of the blossoms and some black pepper. Add the oyster juice and the cream and season with a squeeze of lemon. Let this simmer together a little, but do not reduce. At the last moment, poach the oysters in the sauce. They will cook in 20 to 30 seconds. Cook the pasta and have it ready at the same time as the oysters. Toss the pasta, sauce, and oysters together, and serve garnished with the thyme blossoms all over the top.

Variation: Thyme leaves or other herb blossoms (savory, chervil, sage, and so on) can be used in place of thyme blossoms. Caviar is an appropriate garnish.

Smoked Trout Cappelletti in Fish Soup

1 smoked trout
4 shallots
6 tablespoons sweet butter
3 or 4 sprigs fresh thyme
3 or 4 sprigs fresh chervil
Pepper

1-egg pasta dough
  yield: 40 to 45 cappelletti
2 quarts fish stock
4 tablespoons crème fraîche
Fresh chives

Serves 4

FILET THE TROUT and be careful to remove all the fine little bones. Chop the shallots very fine and stew them in half the butter until they are tender. Finely chop the leaves of the thyme and chervil. Use either a mortar and pestle or a food processor to make a fine paste of the trout. Blend it with the shallots, herbs, and remaining butter. It will probably not need salt because the trout is already salted. Season with black pepper. Roll the pasta and fill the cappelletti (page 13).

BRING THE FISH stock to a boil and simmer the cappelletti gently in the broth until they are cooked. Serve in bowls with the broth, garnished with a dollop of crème fraîche and freshly cut chives. The light fumet is a nice contrast to the aggressive flavor of the smoked trout.

Variations: Use smoked salmon instead of trout, or use smoked chicken or duck in chicken or duck soup. – Reduce cream very slightly and season it with black pepper and lemon juice. Add pieces of very thinly sliced smoked salmon and very thin fettuccine. Toss together and serve garnished with chives, chervil, tarragon, or caviar. Smoked trout can be cooked in the same way.

SUMMER
PASTA

Martine Labro.

Summer is the one time of year when there is good local fresh food everywhere – in your own garden, at farmer's markets, even at the supermarket. It's the season that most evokes the strong flavors of the south of France and the Mediterranean – garlic, tomatoes, peppers, olive oil, anchovies, strong herbs – ingredients that speak for themselves. It's the season for grilling outdoors and cooking informal meals. You can almost plan a menu or a dish by color alone. Summer is a time of bright colors and strong contrasts – red and yellow tomatoes, multicolored peppers, blue and pink hyssop flowers, white and purple variegated eggplants.

Imagine a rambling backyard garden in midsummer – abloom, maybe a little overgrown: the herbs are blossoming, nasturtiums are overflowing their borders, the tomatoes, already heavy with green fruit, are still flowering and sending out new growth. . . . There are inexhaustible choices of little leaves and irresistible flowers to pick and toss into a dish of pasta: thyme and sage blossoms, yellow mustard, wild radish flowers. A summer garden is a cornucopia of pasta possibilities.

July is the month when the California garlic crop is harvested, and the garlic never tastes better than it does right then. It's sweet and pungent and wonderful just stewed a little with some red onions as a pizza topping with some herb flowers scattered on top, or wrapped up in foil with tiny new potatoes and baked until just tender; or raw, in pesto or aïoli. What is more comforting on a hot summer night than a plate of garlicky pasta at midnight to help you sleep? (In addition to its other virtues, garlic is a soporific.) We celebrate every Bastille Day at the restaurant with a big garlic gala and it always serves as a demonstration of why we take the trouble to serve ingredients at their seasonal best. This year we had four different kinds of garlic to use: each had its own qualities and each was at its peak. One year we even organized a garlic tasting, complete with evaluation forms, two judging categories (raw and cooked), double-blind protocols, and a panel of experts.

The pasta recipes in this chapter are all suited to simple menus: sandwiched between two simple, fresh things (a little salad, a bowl of cherries), as first courses followed only by a salad and a little dessert, or just on their own with a glass of rosé. Consider these menus: a dinner starting with red figs, goat cheese, and *mesclun* salad, progressing with pesto lasagne, and ending with apricot and Sauternes ice cream; or a meal of yellow and red tomatoes sliced and dressed with a little olive oil, salt and pepper, and basil flowers, followed by pasta with tuna, olives, lemon, and capers, and a little dessert full of nuts and orange peel; or a lunch of pasta with grilled squid and red onion salad, and a bowl of wild blackberries with sugar; or of pasta with fresh cranberry beans, savory, and garlic, preceded by red and white radishes, and succeeded by baked white peaches; or simply a dish of pasta with Louisiana shrimp and a sauce made from their shells, and for dessert, a compote of cherries and figs.

These are menus that are well served by cold and refreshing uncomplicated wines. The wonderful rosé from Bandol always springs to mind, along with some other Provençal wines – the white wine of Cassis, for example, with its clean taste and hint of lavender. The red wines that find their place on summer menus are usually simpler Chiantis, or lively chilled Beaujolais, or occasionally a robust wine like Zinfandel. But do not rule out the unexpected marriage: an oily California Chardonnay can go remarkably well with tomatoes and strong acid flavors.

HERB FLOWER PASTA

NOT ONLY are herb flowers beautiful, but the flavors are exquisite. They have the characteristic flavor of the herb leaves, but a more delicate version – floral and perfumy. Some even have a nectarlike sweetness. There is a time in the garden when many herbs are flowering simultaneously. In the San Francisco area this is usually near the beginning of July. The exact proportions of herbs in this dish are not important; what matters is freshness and variety.

PLUCK THE BLOSSOMS from all the different herbs you have. Make green pasta with the leaves of thyme, rocket, hyssop, marjoram, basil, sage, parsley, chervil, and sorrel. Chop them very fine and blend into the egg when making the pasta dough. Four or five tablespoons of herbs per egg is a good ratio. Make the pasta in the usual way, roll very thin, and cut into taglierini noodles.

Make an herb butter with minced parsley, chives, chervil, basil, finely diced shallots, butter, salt, and pepper. Cook the herb noodles, and toss with the barely melted butter. Strew the dish of pasta with flowers and serve.

Variations: Serve regular pasta dough, rolled and cut very thin, in a sauce of shallots, cream, and mixed chopped herbs. – Fine noodles sauced with finely chopped fresh mint, cream, salt, and pepper have a delicate flavor. – Or try any single herb in a simple cream sauce.

55

GARDEN SQUASH &
NASTURTIUM BUTTER PASTA

1 teaspoon chopped fresh savory
1 teaspoon chopped fresh thyme
2 teaspoons chopped
  fresh Italian parsley
2 shallots
18 to 20 nasturtiums

4 tablespoons sweet butter
4 tiny yellow squash with flowers
4 tiny zucchini with flowers
½ cup chicken stock
Tagliatelle for 2
Salt and pepper

Serves 2

CHOP ALL of the herbs very fine. Dice the shallots very small. Separate the nasturtium flowers from the stems and chop them. Blend flowers, shallots, and herbs together with the butter and season with salt and pepper. The flavors of the nasturtiums and herbs will permeate the butter if it is made several hours before cooking. Slice the squash into thin rounds and the squash blossoms into ribbons.

USE HALF the butter to gently sauté the squash for 2 or 3 minutes. Add the chicken stock and squash blossoms and simmer while you cook the pasta. Add the tagliatelle and the rest of the nasturtium butter to the squash; season and mix well. The butter sauce is very beautiful on the pasta with all the flecks of color. Serve garnished with additional nasturtium flowers.

Variation: Delicate vegetables that won't overpower the nasturtium butter can be added to or used in place of the squash: whole shallots, fava beans, peas, leeks, and so on.

TAGLIERINI WITH BASIL, GREEN BEANS, & SQUID

1 pound small squid
½ pound tiny green beans
4 or 5 cloves garlic
Several sprigs fresh green and purple basil
½ bunch fresh chives
Salt and pepper
½ cup virgin olive oil
Lemon
Taglierini for 4

Serves 4

CLEAN THE SQUID (see page 183). Cut them lengthwise in narrow strips about the same size as the green beans. Separate the tentacles from the head and leave whole. Rinse the squid thoroughly in cold water. Top and tail the green beans. Peel and finely chop the garlic. Pluck the leaves from the sprigs of green and purple basil and leave them whole. Finely cut the chives.

BLANCH THE GREEN BEANS in the boiling salted pasta water. Remove them while they are still a little crunchy, after 2 to 3 minutes of cooking, and drain. Season the squid with salt and pepper and sauté in 2 tablespoons very hot olive oil in a large pan. In order to remain tender, the squid must be cooked very hot and fast; the total cooking time should be about 2 minutes. When the squid are about half cooked, drop the pasta in the boiling water. Add the garlic, beans, and 5 to 6 tablespoons more oil to the squid. Turn off the flame under the squid as soon as they are cooked. Drain the pasta and add it to the pan along with the basil leaves. Season again with salt and pepper and a squeeze of lemon. Toss all together and serve garnished with chives.

SQUID, PINK PEPPERCORNS, & FETTUCCINE

1½ pounds small squid
6 large shallots
4 red Anaheim peppers
2 tablespoons pink peppercorns
⅔ cup virgin olive oil
Salt and pepper
½ cup Provençal rosé
Fettuccine for 4

Serves 4

CLEAN THE SQUID (see page 183) and slice in very thin rings. Leave the tentacles whole. Peel and thinly slice the shallots. Seed the peppers and cut crosswise in thin rings. Crush the pink peppercorns.

FRY THE SHALLOTS in 2 tablespoons of the olive oil for 2 to 3 minutes. Boost the heat to the highest flame and add the squid. Season with salt and pepper. If the squid are small and thin fleshed, they will cook in 1½ to 2 minutes. Stir frequently while frying. In the last 30 seconds add the rosé wine and crushed pink peppercorns. Have the pasta ready at the same time as the squid and add, along with the remaining olive oil, to the squid. Season with salt, toss all together, and serve immediately.

Variation: Fry tiny artichokes, well trimmed and cut into quarters, in olive oil until tender. Fry strips of squid in hot olive oil and season with salt, pepper, and crushed pink peppercorns. Add a little white wine, some zest and juice of grapefruit, and the artichokes. Toss with the pasta and garnish with chives.

TAGLIATELLE, FRIED SQUID, YELLOW TOMATOES, & GARLIC

8 to 10 small squid
2 large yellow tomatoes
2 cloves garlic
1 shallot
A handful fresh basil and parsley leaves
12 black olives
3 tablespoons virgin olive oil
Crushed red pepper
Salt and pepper
Tagliatelle for 2

Serves 2

CLEAN THE SQUID (see page 183) and cut them in even-sized slices. Peel, seed, and dice the tomatoes. Chop the garlic, shallot, basil, and parsley. Pit the olives and roughly chop them.

SAUTÉ THE GARLIC and shallot in 2 tablespoons olive oil. Add the tomatoes, herbs, and a pinch of crushed red pepper. Season with salt and pepper and simmer a few minutes. Time the cooking of the pasta and the squid so that they are ready at the same time. Season the squid with salt and pepper and sauté it in 1 tablespoon of very hot olive oil. If the squid are small and the flesh fairly thin, they will cook in about 1 minute. Cook over the hottest flame, stirring frequently. When they are done add them to the tomato sauce. Have the pasta ready at the same time; drain and toss it with half of the sauce in a warm serving dish. Serve immediately with the remaining sauce on top, garnished with the black olives.

GRILLED SQUID,
RED ONION, & LINGUINE SALAD

1 pound squid, preferably small
  (about 15 to the pound)
8 to 9 tablespoons
  virgin olive oil
Salt and pepper
1 sweet red onion
Lemon juice
1 golden pepper

A small handful purple basil
  and green basil leaves
10 to 12 Gaeta olives
2 small cloves young garlic
A small handful fresh
  Italian parsley
Red wine vinegar
Linguine for 4

Serves 4

CLEAN THE SQUID (see page 183). Marinate the squid in a little of the olive oil and salt and pepper. Skewer the tentacles on a brochette; they easily fall through the grate if cooked separately. Grill the tentacles and squid bodies over a very hot fire. If they are small, 1½ to 2 minutes on each side will suffice. The flesh when cooked is white and opaque, the skin is pink and spotted. They will shrink to nearly half their original size. Remove them from the grill to a platter and when cool, slice crosswise into thin rings. Leave the tentacles whole. Save the juices that collect on the platter to add to the salad.

Peel and slice the red onion paper thin. Marinate the slices in a teaspoon of lemon juice for 30 minutes or so. Flashfry the onion in a tablespoon of hot olive oil for about 10 seconds. Remove from the pan immediately to stop the cooking and combine with the squid. Season the mixture with salt and pepper. (The brief cooking takes away that raw sharp taste but leaves the onion crisp. If you are fortunate enough to have a really sweet onion that can be eaten raw, this step is not necessary.)

Remove the seeds from the pepper, then slice it in paper-thin rings. Cut the green and purple basil leaves into a chiffonade. Pit the olives and chop them. Mince the garlic and parsley very fine.

COOK THE PASTA, and toss it with the parsley, garlic, 6 to 7 tablespoons of olive oil, and salt and pepper. Combine the pasta, squid, and vegetables. Add vinegar and lemon to taste. The dressing should not be too tart or the sweet squid will be overpowered. Taste for salt and pepper and correct the seasoning. Chill the salad and give it some time for the flavors to blend. This salad is perfect on a hot day with a wine such as Gavi dei Gavi.

Variation: Many combinations of grilled fish and shellfish will make a delicious salad: tuna, scallops, fresh anchovies, shrimp, mussels, lobster, crawfish, and so on.

SQUID, GARLIC, & RED WINE PASTA

1¼ pounds small squid
Salt and pepper
4 shallots
3 or 4 cloves garlic
4 tablespoons chopped fresh thyme and marjoram
½ cup virgin olive oil
1 cup Italian Chianti
Fettuccine for 4
Thyme blossoms

Serves 4

CLEAN THE SQUID (see page 183). Cut the squid crosswise into very thin rings. Combine the tentacles with the rings and season with salt and pepper. Chop the shallots, garlic, and herbs very fine and mix them together.

THE SQUID COOKS very fast, about 1½ minutes in all. In a large sauté pan, heat 2 to 3 tablespoons of the olive oil until almost smoking hot. Sauté the squid, stirring frequently. After 30 seconds or so, add the shallots, garlic, and herb mixture. When the squid is almost cooked, the skin will turn pink and the flesh an opaque white. Add the rest of the olive oil and the Chianti and cook another 20 seconds or so. Have the pasta ready at the same time as the squid and add to the pan. Remove from the heat and mix well. The wine color of the sauce looks beautiful with the pink of the squid. Serve garnished with additional black pepper and thyme blossoms.

Note: The inspiration for this dish comes from Richard Olney's recipe for Squid and Leeks in Red Wine in his book *Simple French Food* (New York: Atheneum, 1974). It is a deep and savory stew that we have often served over pasta at the restaurant.

GRILLED SUMMER VEGETABLE PASTA

2 salt-packed anchovies
Virgin olive oil
3 peppers – yellow, green, red
6 to 8 small Japanese eggplants
Salt and pepper
8 plum tomatoes
1 young red onion
1 or 2 cloves garlic
A few fresh basil leaves
Tagliatelle for 2

Serves 2

FILET AND RINSE the anchovies. Pound them in a mortar with a little olive oil to make a smooth paste. Make a charcoal fire. While the charcoal is still flaming, grill the peppers so that the skin is black and blistered all around. Let them cool and peel away the charred skin. Cut in half lengthwise and remove the seeds and stem. Use a paring knife or a towel to remove any little bits of black on the exterior, then cut the peppers into wide strips. Cut the unpeeled eggplants in lengthwise slices about ¼-inch thick. Brush the slices with olive oil and season with salt and pepper. Grill them over the hot fire a few minutes on each side so that they are lightly browned. Cut the plum tomatoes in half and season with salt and pepper. Grill them skin side down until they get a little color and begin to soften. Slice the onion in rings. Brush with olive oil, season, and grill them until browned and tender. Finely chop the garlic. Cut the basil leaves into a chiffonade.

COMBINE THE ANCHOVY paste, tomato halves, garlic, and a tablespoon of oil in a sauté pan. Cook gently a few minutes until the tomatoes release their juices and form a sauce. Add the grilled vegetables and continue to simmer a few minutes more. Cook the pasta and add to the vegetables. Season with black pepper and toss the noodles well in the juices. Serve garnished with all the vegetables and the chiffonade of basil.

63

EGGPLANT, PEPPER, & PASTA SALAD

2 medium eggplants	Red wine vinegar
Salt	1½ pounds cherry tomatoes
Light olive oil for frying	3 to 4 tablespoons
4 or 5 different-colored peppers	virgin olive oil
4 sweet, long Italian peppers	A handful chopped
2 cloves garlic	fresh Italian parsley
2 handfuls fresh basil leaves	Whole-wheat spaghetti for 8
Pepper	

Serves 8

THIS SALAD is best if made a day before serving and allowed to marinate. Cut the eggplant into round slices approximately ⅛-inch thick. Sprinkle with salt and let them sweat for 30 minutes or so, then pat dry with a towel. Deep fry the slices, a few at a time, in very hot olive oil (375°F if you have a thermometer), until nicely browned on both sides. Drain and set aside.

Roast the colored peppers. Peel and seed them and cut into wide strips. If they have not cooked sufficiently during the roasting, sauté in a little olive oil until soft. Slice the long Italian peppers into very thin rounds. Mince the garlic very fine. Pluck the basil leaves. Cut the very large ones into narrow strips and leave the small ones whole.

Combine the peppers, basil, and garlic. Season with salt and pepper, then sprinkle liberally with vinegar and mix well. In a shallow dish layer the eggplant slices, lightly seasoned with salt, and cover with peppers. Add another layer of eggplant, then peppers, and so on. (The purpose of layering the vegetables instead of mixing everything together is to avoid tearing the fragile eggplant; the salad will then look beautiful when served.) Refrigerate it overnight. Before serving, taste for vinegar and salt, adding more if necessary.

Purée the tomatoes through a food mill or a sieve to extract the juice. Mix with a few tablespoons of the virgin olive oil and chopped parsley. Cook the spaghetti, drain, and dress with the tomato juice and oil; chill. Serve on a large platter with the spaghetti piled high in the center surrounded by the eggplant and pepper salad.

Variation: Use regular pasta or dried fusilli with toasted bread crumbs tossed in olive oil as a garnish.

FRIED BREAD & FUSILLI SALAD

4 cups fresh bread crumbs
12 ripe tomatoes
Several sprigs fresh thyme
A handful fresh basil leaves
A large bouquet fresh parsley
Salt and pepper
3 or 4 cloves garlic
½ cup virgin olive oil
½ pound dried fusilli

Serves 4

A PASTA SALAD is probably the best way to describe this dish. The sauce is not cooked and it is meant to be eaten tepid. The spiral shape of the fusilli is important because it holds the sauce in just the right way, but the most important ingredient in the dish is a flavorful bread. The sort that is wanted is a country-style bread made from a mixture of flours – a crusty slow-baked loaf. Cut the crust from the bread and use a blender, food processor, or grater to make coarse bread crumbs. Put the bread crumbs on a baking sheet and bake in a slow oven until they are dry and crisp but not brown. Peel, seed, and finely chop the tomatoes. Finely chop all of the herbs, mix them with the tomatoes, and season with salt and pepper. Mince the garlic. Heat the olive oil in a skillet and add the bread crumbs and garlic; stir constantly over medium heat until they are golden brown. Pour them into a bowl and set aside.

Cook the pasta al dente, drain, and put it in a large serving dish. Toss well with the tomatoes and herbs. Add the bread crumbs, toss well again, and serve.

65

LINGUINE WITH
CHERRY TOMATO VINAIGRETTE

5 cups cherry tomatoes, preferably Sweet 100
1 cup virgin olive oil
Red wine vinegar
Salt and pepper
1½ cups fresh bread crumbs
A handful fresh basil leaves
Linguine for 4

Serves 4

THE QUALITY of this simple pasta depends on the excellence of the tomatoes. (Sweet 100 is a varietal name. They are very small and intensely sweet.) Cut the tomatoes in half and marinate them in olive oil, red wine vinegar to taste, and salt and pepper. Toast the fresh bread crumbs in the oven until dry and lightly browned. Take them from the oven and toss with some olive oil while still warm. Cut the basil leaves into tiny ribbons. Cook the pasta, and while it is boiling, put the tomatoes in a pan and warm them. Add the pasta to the pan, toss together with the tomatoes, and serve. Garnish the dish with the bread crumbs and basil chiffonade.

Variations: Peel large ripe tomatoes and quarter them. Dress them with virgin olive oil, red wine vinegar, salt and pepper, minced garlic, and lots of dwarf basil leaves. Cook fresh noodles and toss the hot pasta with the cold tomatoes. – Finely dice peeled and seeded tomatoes, a mixture of multicolored sweet peppers, and red onion. Season with salt, pepper, vinegar, and chopped parsley, basil, and coriander. Boil linguine, drain, toss in olive oil, then mix with the relish and chill.

TOMATO & CHEESE LASAGNE

Tomato Sauce:
7 large tomatoes
1 red torpedo onion
4 cloves garlic
3 to 4 tablespoons virgin olive oil
1 tablespoon tomato paste
1 bay leaf
Several sprigs each fresh thyme, basil, parsley
Crushed red pepper
A section of prosciutto bone

¼ pound Parmesan
½ pound mozzarella
2 sprigs fresh marjoram with flowers
1 cup ricotta
A small handful fresh basil leaves
A small handful fresh Italian parsley
Black pepper
2-egg pasta dough

Serves 6

THE TOMATO SAUCE is sweet, simmered slowly, and puréed to a very smooth texture. The quantities of cheeses, sauce, and pasta listed above will fill a dish 10 by 6 by 2 inches.

To make the sauce, peel, seed, and chop the tomatoes. Dice the onion and mince the garlic, then sauté in olive oil for a few minutes. Add the tomatoes, tomato paste, bay leaf, chopped herbs, a pinch of crushed red pepper, and a section of prosciutto bone. Simmer gently for about an hour and a half. Remove the bone, purée the sauce through a food mill, and taste for seasoning. The prosciutto should provide enough of both salt and pepper. Grate the Parmesan and mozzarella. Keep them separate. Pluck the flowers from sprigs of marjoram and add to the ricotta. Finely chop the basil and Italian parsley and add to the ricotta. Season with some ground black pepper.

68

ROLL, CUT, AND PARBOIL the pasta (see page 12). Layer the lasagne in this way: Put a light layer of sauce on the bottom of the dish. Cover with a sheet of pasta and spread it with sauce. Sprinkle with grated mozzarella and Parmesan. Cover with another sheet of pasta and sauce. Put half of the ricotta and herb mixture on this layer. Repeat with a layer of pasta, sauce, and mozzarella and Parmesan, then another layer of pasta, topped with the remaining ricotta. Make one more layer of pasta and mozzarella and Parmesan, and end with a top layer of pasta and sauce and Parmesan. Cover the lasagne with foil and bake 20 minutes in a 350°F oven. Remove the foil and bake another 20 minutes or so, until the top is crusty and golden.

PASTA WITH PESTO

4 cloves young garlic, or 2 cloves mature garlic
½ teaspoon coarse sea salt
Whole black peppercorns
2 cups roughly chopped fresh basil leaves
⅓ cup virgin olive oil
¼ cup lightly toasted pine nuts
⅓ cup grated Parmesan and pecorino, mixed
Linguine for 4 to 6

Serves 4 to 6

SLICE THE GARLIC and put it in a mortar with the coarse sea salt and a few black peppercorns. Begin to pound with the pestle and add a small handful of basil leaves and a tablespoon or so of olive oil. Continue to add more leaves gradually, along with a little olive oil and some pine nuts. Keep pounding and adding until all of the basil and nuts are in the mortar. You will only have used about half the oil at this point. Too much oil will make it difficult to grind the ingredients to a paste. When you have worked the mixture into a smooth paste, stir in the freshly grated cheeses and the remaining oil. Taste for salt and add more if needed. Let the pesto rest a little while for the flavors to marry.

Use a few tablespoons of pesto for each serving of pasta. Put the pesto in a warm bowl or pan and add a little of the boiling pasta water to it, then add the hot pasta and toss well to coat the noodles. A narrow noodle such as linguine or taglierini is well matched with pesto. The sauce will keep for several days if refrigerated.

PESTO, NEW POTATOES, & PASTA

5 or 6 new potatoes
Olive oil
Salt and pepper
Fresh thyme leaves
Linguine for 4
1 recipe pesto sauce (page 70)
Parmesan

Serves 4

WASH THE NEW POTATOES; leave the skins on. Cut the potatoes in thin slices, then toss them in olive oil in a baking dish. Season with salt and pepper, add some fresh thyme leaves, and roast them in a hot oven. Turn and stir the potatoes a few times during the cooking so that they brown evenly. When they are brown and crisp, remove them from the oven to a warm serving dish. Cook the linguine and toss with the potatoes and pesto. Serve immediately with freshly grated Parmesan at the table.

71

PESTO LASAGNE

Pesto:
5 or 6 cloves young garlic or 3 or 4 cloves mature garlic
Coarse salt
Whole black peppercorns
4 cups roughly chopped fresh basil leaves
¾ cup virgin olive oil
⅓ cup lightly toasted pine nuts
⅔ cup Parmesan and pecorino mixed

Béchamel Sauce:
3 tablespoons butter
3 tablespoons all-purpose flour
3 cups half-and-half
1 cup heavy cream
Salt and pepper
Nutmeg
Bouquet garni
  (thyme, parsley, bay leaf,
  black peppercorns, onion, and garlic)

2-egg pasta dough
⅓ cup Parmesan and bread crumbs
2 tablespoons sweet butter

Serves 6

MAKE THE PESTO in a mortar according to the directions on page 70. To make the béchamel sauce, melt the butter in a saucepan, and when it is gently foaming add the flour and whisk together. Cook the roux over low heat for 5 minutes or so, stirring frequently with a wooden spoon. Be careful not to let the flour brown. Turn off the heat and let it cool a little. Combine the half-and-half and cream and heat them almost to the boiling point. Pour them into the roux, in a steady stream, whisking all the while until the mixture is smooth. Season with salt and pepper and a subtle amount of nutmeg. Make a bouquet garni of a few sprigs each of thyme and parsley, a bay leaf, a few black peppercorns, a slice or two of onion, and 3 or 4 cloves garlic. Wrap these ingredients in a piece of cheesecloth and tie it with string. Put the bouquet garni and the béchamel in the top of a double boiler, cover, and let it simmer for an hour or so, stirring occasionally as it cooks. Remove it from the heat and let it cool while you roll and cook the pasta (see page 12 for the method of constructing the lasagne).

Remove the bouquet garni from the béchamel and blend the two sauces together. Layer the thin sheets of pasta with a light, even coating of sauce; repeat with layers of pasta and sauce until the dish is filled. These quantities will fill a dish approximately 12 by 9 by 2 inches. Finish the lasagne, folding the last sheets together like a package. Cover the top with a layer of freshly grated Parmesan and fresh bread crumbs and dot with butter. Cover with foil and bake in a 350°F oven for 15 to 20 minutes, then remove the foil and bake another 15 minutes, or until the cheese and bread crumb top is golden brown. Let the lasagne cool just a little before serving. The aroma is irresistible.

GREEN & RED PASTA

Green Sauce:
3 cups fresh basil leaves
¾ cup virgin olive oil
3 or 4 cloves garlic
Salt and pepper
¼ cup capers
¼ cup pine nuts
Fresh purple basil leaves

Red Sauce:
3 large ripe tomatoes
Salt and pepper
3 to 4 tablespoons virgin olive oil
1 sweet red pepper
2 salt-packed anchovies
2 or 3 cloves garlic

Tagliatelle for 6
Leaves of Italian parsley

Serves 6

TO MAKE THE GREEN SAUCE: Purée the basil leaves with the olive oil in a food processor or blender. Pound the garlic in a mortar to a smooth paste and blend it with the basil oil. Season with salt and pepper to taste. Rinse the capers in cold water to remove the brine. Lightly toast the pine nuts. The capers, pine nuts, and purple basil leaves are added to the pasta just at the end.

To make the red sauce: Core the tomatoes and cut them in half crosswise. Remove the seeds, salt and pepper them, and brush with some olive oil. Grill the tomatoes, 5 minutes or so on each side, over a wood or charcoal fire. Grill the red pepper over the hottest part of the fire until the skin completely blackens. While the peppers cool, skin the tomatoes and roughly chop them. Peel the skin from the pepper and remove the core and seeds. Finely chop the pepper and mix with the tomatoes. Rinse and filet the anchovies and pound them in a mortar with the garlic to a smooth paste. Blend the paste and tomatoes, add the rest of the olive oil, and season with black pepper.

HAVE THE SAUCES ready in two separate bowls. Cook the pasta and mix half with the green sauce and half with the red. Serve them side by side on a warm serving platter. Garnish the green pasta with the capers, pine nuts, and leaves of purple basil. Garnish the red pasta with leaves of Italian parsley. And of course, serve Green and Red Zinfandel from Jay Heminway's winery in Napa Valley.

Variations: Some other possibilities for pairs of sauces are tapenade and tomato sauce; anchovy cream and a home-dried tomato purée with herbs and olive oil; grilled tomato sauce and a sauce made with poutargue (smoked fish roe): work the roe with pepper, lemon juice, and olive oil so it makes an emulsion like mayonnaise.

LOUISIANA SHRIMP SAUCE & FETTUCCINE

1 pound whole shrimp	A few sprigs fresh thyme
2 shallots	1 pound ripe tomatoes
4 cloves garlic	4 tablespoons olive oil
1 carrot	Salt and pepper
1 onion	A pinch of cayenne
1 stalk celery	¾ cup dry white wine
A large handful	1 cup water
fresh basil leaves	Lemon
A few sprigs fresh parsley	Fettuccine for 2

Serves 2

WASH THE SHRIMP and remove the heads, shells, and tails. Peel and dice the shallots and the garlic and save half of each for the final cooking of the shrimp. Finely dice the carrot, onion, and celery. Save half of the basil for the garnish, cutting it into thin ribbons, and put the rest with the vegetables. Roughly chop the parsley and thyme. Chop the tomatoes and keep them separate from the other vegetables.

Make the sauce. Fry the shrimp heads and shells in 2 tablespoons very hot olive oil for a minute or so, until they turn pink and are very lightly browned. Add the diced vegetables, including half the garlic and shallots, and the herbs. Season with salt, pepper, and a pinch of cayenne, then sauté for 2 or 3 minutes, stirring frequently. Deglaze the pan by adding the wine, and scrape the bottom with a wooden spoon. Let the wine cook down a little, then add the tomatoes. When the tomatoes begin to soften and release their juices, add the water. Let the whole simmer briskly for 30 or 40 minutes. Stir frequently and use the wooden spoon to mash the heads and shells to extract the maximum amount of flavor from them.

Strain the sauce through a sieve, using a wooden spoon to press all of the liquid out of the shells and vegetables. There will be approximately 2 cups of sauce. Reduce it gently by about half.

SAUTÉ THE SHRIMP in the remaining 2 tablespoons hot olive oil. Season with salt, pepper, and a squeeze of lemon. After a minute or so, lower the heat and add the reserved garlic and shallots. Cook another minute and add the sauce. Taste for seasoning; it might want more salt, lemon, or cayenne. Cook the pasta, and toss it with the sauce. Serve garnished with the chiffonade of basil.

TAGLIATELLE, FRIED PRAWNS, GARLIC, & PARSLEY

2 pounds prawns
4 or 5 cloves garlic
2 handfuls fresh parsley leaves
6 to 8 tablespoons virgin olive oil
Salt and pepper
Tagliatelle for 4
Lemon

Serves 4

THIS IS an extremely simple pasta. Its quality depends upon the freshness of the prawns. The excellent California prawns from the Santa Barbara area number approximately 25 to the pound.

Rinse the prawns well in cold water and remove the heads and shells. Chop the garlic and parsley very fine.

SAUTÉ THE PRAWNS in a few tablespoons of the hot olive oil. Season with salt and pepper. When they are nearly cooked, after about 2 minutes, lower the heat (if the oil is too hot when the garlic is added it will brown and its flavor will be too strong) and add the garlic, parsley, and 5 or 6 more tablespoons olive oil. Cook the pasta and add to the prawns. Toss well, season with a squeeze of lemon juice, and serve.

SALMON & ROASTED RED PEPPER PASTA

½ pound salmon
3 shallots
Several sprigs fresh parsley
6 tablespoons light olive oil
1 lemon
3 sweet red peppers

Several sprigs fresh basil
6 green onions
1 cup fresh bread crumbs
4 tablespoons virgin olive oil
Salt and pepper
Fettuccine for 4

Serves 4

REMOVE ALL THE BONES and skin from the salmon and cut into small thin slices. Dice the shallots and chop the parsley. Marinate these ingredients together with some light olive oil and the juice of half a lemon. Roast, peel, and seed the peppers. Cut them into thin strips and dress with some of the olive oil and a chiffonade of basil leaves. Trim the green onions and cut them into a long julienne. Toast the bread crumbs until dry and lightly browned, then toss with a little virgin olive oil.

SAUTÉ THE PEPPERS and green onions in a little olive oil for 1 to 2 minutes until the onions have softened. Cook the fettuccine. Add the salmon to the peppers and continue to cook another 1 to 2 minutes until the fish is just done. Do not let the salmon overcook and become dry. Season with salt and pepper and more lemon juice to taste. Add the cooked fettuccine and mix all together. Serve garnished with the crunchy bread crumbs.

Tuna with Olives,
Lemon, Capers, & Tagliatelle

½ pound tuna filet
1 small lemon
2 cloves garlic
2 dozen Nicoise olives
Several sprigs fresh parsley
1 tablespoon capers
½ cup virgin olive oil
Salt and pepper
Tagliatelle for 2

Serves 2

CUT THE PIECE of fresh tuna filet into small slices about ¼-inch thick. Slice the ends off the lemon and carefully cut down the sides, removing the peel and all of the white pith. Slice the lemon into rounds and cut the rounds into quarters. Peel and chop the garlic. Pit the olives and coarsely chop them. Finely chop the parsley leaves. Rinse the capers well under running water to remove the taste of the brine.

SAUTÉ THE TUNA in hot olive oil. Season it with salt and pepper and add the garlic, lemon, olives, and capers. Reduce the heat. The fish will cook very quickly, about 2 minutes in all; watch carefully that it does not overcook or it will be dry. While the tuna is cooking, cook the pasta, then add the tagliatelle and parsley to the tuna and toss all together well. Taste for salt and serve garnished with freshly ground black pepper.

Variation: Substitute salmon for tuna or try it with smoked chicken. Do not actually cook the smoked chicken; add it with the pasta to the warm olive oil and garlic, lemon, and so on.

FRESH CRANBERRY BEANS, SAVORY, OLIVE OIL, & FETTUCCINE

3 pounds young fresh cranberry
beans (about 3 cups shelled)
1 red onion
1 stalk celery
8 cloves garlic
2 slices bacon
2 slices pancetta
1 sprig fresh thyme
4 sprigs fresh savory

1 bay leaf
6 to 7 tablespoons
virgin olive oil
Salt and pepper
3½ cups chicken stock
A small bunch fresh parsley
Parmesan
Fettuccine for 4

Serves 4

SHELL THE BEANS. Dice the red onion and celery. Peel and chop the garlic. Cut the bacon and pancetta slices into small pieces. Chop the leaves of a sprig each of thyme and savory. Sauté the onion, celery, bacon, pancetta, and half the garlic in 2 tablespoons olive oil for 8 to 10 minutes. Add the beans and herbs, season with salt and pepper, and continue cooking a few minutes more. Heat the chicken stock and add 3 cups to the beans and bring to a boil. Simmer the beans for approximately 45 minutes, until they are soft but not mushy. Purée half the beans and return the purée to the pot with another ½ cup of chicken stock. Taste for salt and bring to a gentle simmer again.

Make a little sauce of 4 to 5 tablespoons olive oil, the parsley, chopped, 3 sprigs of finely chopped savory, and the rest of the minced garlic. Cook the pasta, drain it, and mix into the pot of beans. Serve very hot, garnished with ground black pepper, and with the garlic and herb sauce poured over the top. Pass around freshly grated Parmesan at the table.

SUMMER VEGETABLE RAGOÛT PASTA

1 sweet red pepper	2 large ripe tomatoes
1 green pepper	Several sprigs fresh
1 sweet red onion	basil, parsley, and marjoram
5 or 6 mushrooms	½ cup virgin olive oil
3 or 4 cloves garlic	Salt and pepper
3 small zucchini squash	1 cup chicken stock
2 small summer squash	Lemon
2 small crookneck squash	2 tablespoons sweet butter
1 handful tiny green beans	Fettuccine for 4
7 or 8 small carrots	Leaves of purple basil (optional)

Serves 4

MANY COMBINATIONS of vegetables will make an interesting ragoût, especially if you have a garden and can pick a mixture of everything you have growing. These ingredients provide a variety of textures, flavors, and colors, which is the essence of this dish.

Wash and prepare all of the vegetables. Core, seed, and thinly slice the peppers, and thinly slice the onion. Quarter the mushrooms. Mince the garlic. Thinly slice the squashes. Top and tail the green beans. Peel and julienne the carrots. Peel, seed, and dice the tomatoes. Chop the herbs, and keep the parsley separate for the garnish.

SAUTÉ THE ONIONS and mushrooms in ¼ cup olive oil for 3 to 4 minutes. Add the peppers and half the garlic, season with salt and pepper, and cook another 2 to 3 minutes. Add the squashes, tomatoes, basil, and marjoram. Season again with salt. Add the warm chicken stock and cook over a high flame for 2 to 3 minutes more while you parboil the green beans and carrots. Boil them for just a minute or so, then remove and add to the other vegetables. Add another ¼ cup olive oil, the remaining garlic, and a squeeze of lemon juice. Taste the broth for salt and lemon. Remove from the heat and stir in 2 tablespoons butter to enrich the sauce. Cook the fettuccine and place in warm serving bowls. Serve the colorful ragoût over the pasta. Garnish with chopped parsley, black pepper, and, if you have it, leaves of purple basil.

Note: This is another dish created by Richard Olney. In his book, *Simple French Food* (New York: Atheneum, 1974), he gives a fine recipe

81

for vegetable stew as well as a thorough discourse on various possible ingredients, and methods of combining them. Each season can inspire a new composition of vegetables with the constant of onions, mushrooms, tomatoes, and olive oil as the base of the ragoût and sauce.

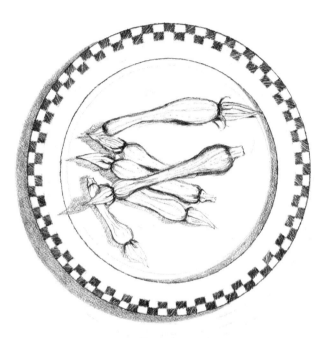

FALL
PASTA

Martine Lafon

Fall is the transitional season. The luxuriant abundance of the late summer starts to wane, but there's still a feeling of amplitude and plenty. Just a list of the foods harvested in the fall can evoke vivid memories of a snap in the air, Indian summer sunsets, and falling leaves: pumpkins, walnuts, chestnuts, grapes, apples, pears. . . . I feel like spending more time at the table and the fare gets a little richer. More animal fat makes its way into meals: ducks and geese, fresh and preserved; pork and charcuterie; and if we're lucky, game birds, venison, and wild boar. Good shellfish starts to reappear, and wild mushrooms are at their peak. White truffles come to us from Italy, and boletes, chanterelles, blewits, Lepiotas, and many more are available locally.

The recipes in this chapter include reworkings of some familiar pasta dishes. There is a swan song for late-season tomatoes (grilled tomato sauce), several recipes for pasta with clams, and a version of spaghetti and meatballs that I hope dispels any unpleasant childhood meatball memories.

These autumnal menus really appeal to me: Sunday dinner with a roasted red pepper salad, roast chicken with pumpkin ravioli, and apple pie, sounds comforting and familial. Another menu might begin with pasta with oysters, fennel, and cream, and continue with an escarole salad, and a quince compote. A Provençal dinner can be made of marinated sardines, pasta with grilled radicchio and pancetta, and frosted muscat grapes. For an extremely elegant supper I love white truffle pasta followed by roast wild duck, with pears and Gorgonzola for dessert. For an extremely simple lunch, gather up the last of your garden's lettuces, maybe a little tough and beginning to bolt, wilt them, and toss them into a dish of peppery pasta.

Every November at Chez Panisse we celebrate a Zinfandel Festival. For almost ten years our friends at Joseph Phelps Vineyard in the Napa Valley have been making us new Zinfandel from the grapes picked a month or two before that same fall. Like Beaujolais Nouveau, it is fruity, light, and promotes a good deal of hilarity. Just such a wine serves well for many fall pastas. Other dishes may call for nobler vintages. Wild mushrooms, for example, are particularly good with fine old Bordeaux. Alsatian wines seem to go well with autumnal cooking, too. Try drinking an Alsatian Riesling with clam pasta. Or match an old Italian vintage with white truffle pasta.

BUCKWHEAT PASTA,
ROASTED PEPPERS, & ENDIVE

2 sweet red peppers
2 leeks
2 Belgian endives
4 chanterelles
1 clove garlic
3 slices bacon
½ cup virgin olive oil
Salt and pepper
Buckwheat taglierini for 4

Serves 4

ROAST THE PEPPERS and peel and seed them. Cut the peppers, leeks, and endive leaves into a julienne. Thinly slice the chanterelles and finely chop the garlic. Cut the bacon in small strips; cook until lightly browned, then drain, and set aside.

Stew the leeks in ¼ cup olive oil. After a few minutes, when the leeks are soft, add the mushrooms and garlic. Season with salt and pepper and sauté a few minutes. Add the endive, bacon, and red peppers and continue to cook a few minutes more, until the endive has wilted. Cook the pasta and add to the pan with the remaining ¼ cup olive oil. Season with black pepper, toss all together and serve with:

Chicken Breasts with Olives & Bread Crumbs

Trim the boned chicken breasts of all fat and sinew. Melt a few tablespoons of butter and mix it with a few tablespoons of olive paste. Dip the chicken breasts in this mixture, then roll in fresh bread crumbs. Fry gently in a little clarified butter until the chicken is nicely browned and just cooked.

HOT RED SAUSAGE,
RED PEPPERS, & WHOLE-WHEAT PASTA

¾ pound spicy hot sausage
3 sweet red peppers
4 small leeks
2 or 3 cloves garlic
Parmesan and pepato (optional)
2 to 3 tablespoons chopped fresh parsley
4 to 5 tablespoons virgin olive oil
½ cup chicken stock
Whole-wheat tagliatelle for 4
Salt and pepper

Serves 4

A CALABRIAN STYLE of sausage is the main ingredient of this pasta. It is made with pork and beef, mainly pork. The seasoning is fennel seed, black pepper, garlic, and quite a lot of red pepper. The cayenne pepper, some of it crushed to a powder and some in large flakes, actually makes the sausage a bright red color, an indication of the heat of the flavor.

Pepato is an Italian aged sheep's-milk cheese made with whole black peppercorns in the center. It has a very dry sharp flavor.

Slice the sausage into rounds. Seed the peppers and cut them into thin slices. Cut the white parts of the leeks in half lengthwise, rinse in water, and slice thin. Peel and chop the garlic. Grate the two cheeses and mix them together. Chop the parsley.

SAUTÉ THE SAUSAGE in a few tablespoons of olive oil. After 5 minutes or so, when it is half cooked, add the leeks, red peppers, and garlic. When all are cooked, about another 5 minutes, add a few more tablespoons olive oil and the chicken stock. Cook the pasta, then add to the sausage and peppers. Mix everything together and taste for salt and pepper. Serve garnished with the two cheeses and parsley.

Variation: A pasta with a Moroccan flavor can be made with grilled or fried merguez (spicy lamb sausages), fried peppers and baby onions, garlic, salted and preserved lemon, whole blanched almonds, tomatoes, and Bandol Tempier Rosé.

90

RADICCHIO, PANCETTA, & BUCKWHEAT NOODLES

1 head radicchio
2 salt-packed anchovies
3 green onions
4 slices pancetta
2 cloves garlic
½ cup virgin olive oil
¾ cup reduced bird stock
  (pigeon, duck, or chicken)

Buckwheat tagliatelle for 4
Red wine vinegar
Salt and pepper
Toasted fresh bread crumbs
Grated dry jack cheese

Serves 4

CUT THE RADICCHIO in half, remove the core, and cut into a very fine chiffonade. Filet, rinse, and finely chop the anchovies. Cut the green onions into a julienne and blanch briefly in boiling salted water. Slice the pancetta in small pieces, sauté until lightly browned, and drain. Peel and finely chop the garlic.

WARM THE OLIVE OIL, anchovy, and garlic in a large sauté pan. Add the radicchio chiffonade and cook briefly. Heat the stock in a small pan; add to the sauté pan, bring up the heat and add the green onions and pancetta. Let this simmer together while the pasta cooks. Drain the noodles and add to the pan. Toss all together and add a splash of red wine vinegar. Taste for salt and pepper. Serve garnished with toasted bread crumbs and grated dry jack cheese.

Variation: Grill the radicchio. Cut the head in quarters, brush with olive oil, season, and cook over a low fire. Grill the pancetta slices, then cut them in small pieces. After it is grilled, cut the radicchio into a fine chiffonade and proceed with the recipe.

GORGONZOLA MASCARPONE & LINGUINE

⅓ cup heavy cream
4 ounces Gorgonzola mascarpone
Linguine for 2
Toasted nuts
Black pepper

Serves 2

HEAT THE CREAM, add the cheese, and simmer gently until it is melted. Cook the pasta, add to the sauce, and mix well to coat the noodles. The sauce is better if not thick and reduced, for it will thicken of its own as it cools at the table. Toasted nuts make an excellent garnish: walnuts roasted in the oven, almonds sautéed in olive oil, toasted pistachios or pecans. Garnish with freshly ground black pepper and serve with a good red wine.

Variations: Gorgonzola mascarpone is actually an aged, veined cheese and fresh cream cheese layered together. You can use Gorgonzola alone, in place of the mascarpone. How much to use depends upon the strength of flavor of the cheese. This can vary a great deal from firm and underripe to an off-color, bitter, ammoniated, and overripe cheese. Taste before you buy, for a soft, creamy, full-flavored Gorgonzola. – Or make a three-cheese pasta: a blend of Gorgonzola, aged fontina, Parmesan, and cream.

SCALLOPS & ROASTED PEPPER PASTA

1 pound bay scallops	2 cups fresh bread crumbs
Salt and pepper	Virgin olive oil
All-purpose flour	¼ cup olive oil
2 sweet red peppers or pimentos	1 or 2 cloves garlic, chopped
2 leeks	Lemon juice
2 sprigs fresh thyme	1 cup chicken stock
A small bunch fresh parsley	Tagliatelle for 4

Serves 4

TRIM AWAY the tough little muscle on the side of the scallops. Season the scallops with salt and pepper and flour lightly. Roast, peel, and seed the peppers. Cut the peppers and leeks into a julienne. Blanch the leeks briefly in boiling water. Finely chop the thyme and parsley. Toast fresh bread crumbs in the oven until dry and lightly browned, then toss them in some virgin olive oil.

SAUTÉ THE SCALLOPS in very hot olive oil. When they are just browned, but not fully cooked, add the garlic. Remove from the pan, sprinkle with chopped thyme and parsley, season with lemon juice, and set aside while finishing the sauce. Deglaze the pan with the chicken stock and reduce by half. Then add the peppers and leeks. Lower the heat and add the scallops. Let them simmer the minute or so it takes to cook the pasta. Add the noodles to the pan and toss all together. Taste for salt and pepper. Serve garnished with the toasted bread crumbs. Serve a little dish of the bread crumbs at the table as you would grated cheese.

CLAMS, BACON, OLIVE OIL, & LINGUINE

1½ pounds small tender clams
3 small leeks
Several sprigs fresh parsley
4 cloves garlic
1 bay leaf
Several sprigs fresh thyme

3 slices bacon
4 to 5 tablespoons
 virgin olive oil
Pepper
A pinch of crushed red pepper
Green linguine for 2

Serves 2

SCRUB THE CLAMS under cold running water. Put them in a large pot with the tops of the leeks, washed well and sliced, the parsley stems, 2 crushed garlic cloves, a bay leaf, and a few tablespoons water. Cover the pot and steam open the clams. Stop the cooking as soon as they begin to open. Remove the lid and let them cool.

Cut the white part of the leeks in half lengthwise. Wash them well in cold water and slice thin. Peel and chop 2 cloves of garlic. Remove the leaves from 2 or 3 sprigs of thyme. Chop the leaves of several sprigs of parsley. Cut the bacon slices into small pieces. Take the clams out of their shells and set aside. Strain the clam juices and set aside.

START THE LEEKS and garlic cooking in a few tablespoons of the olive oil. Season with ground black pepper and add the thyme leaves. Cook gently for 5 minutes or so and then add approximately ½ cup of the clam juice, and a pinch of crushed red pepper flakes. Meanwhile, in a separate pan, fry the bacon pieces until lightly browned. Add 2 or 3 more tablespoons of olive oil to the leeks and add the clams. This should be done just at the last moment so the clams do not undergo further cooking but are merely heated. Cook the linguine and add to the pan. Add the bacon pieces, season with ground black pepper, and toss well. Serve in bowls with the pan juices and garnish with chopped parsley.

Variation: Steam open the clams and make a sauce with virgin olive oil, chopped garlic, and the juices. At the last moment, add the clams, a pinch of crushed red pepper, and the linguine. Garnish with black pepper and chopped parsley.

CLAMS, GREMOLATA, & LINGUINE

3 pounds small tender clams
  (approximately 20 per pound)
Chopped onion or shallot
A small bunch fresh
  Italian parsley
1 sprig fresh thyme
1 bay leaf

White wine
2 or 3 cloves garlic
1 small lemon
1 cup heavy cream
Linguine for 4
Pepper

Serves 4

WASH THE CLAMS thoroughly. Steam them open in a covered pot with a little chopped onion or shallot, the parsley stems, a sprig of thyme, a bay leaf, and a little white wine. Cook over high heat until they just open; be careful not to overcook or they will toughen. Remove them from the pot, allow to cool, and take them out of their shells. Let the sand settle to the bottom of the juices, and then carefully pour off the liquid through a strainer. Reserve about 1 cup.

To make the gremolata, finely chop the parsley leaves and garlic cloves. Grate the lemon rind very fine, and mix the three together.

COMBINE 1 CUP cream and approximately 1 cup clam juice (depending on how salty it is) and simmer together. While the pasta is boiling, add the clams and half the gremolata to the sauce. Do not allow the clams to cook any further, just heat through. Add the noodles and toss well. Season with black pepper and serve garnished with the remaining gremolata sprinkled on top.

Variation: Try this recipe with saffron pasta and mussels, or a combination of mussels and clams.

CLAMS, MIREPOIX VEGETABLES, & LINGUINE

1½ pounds steamer clams
Shallots
Several sprigs fresh parsley
1 bay leaf
Garlic
White wine
2 carrots

2 stalks celery
1 onion
2 tablespoons sweet butter
½ cup heavy cream
Linguine for 2
Pepper

Serves 2

SOAK AND SCRUB the clams in several changes of fresh water. Steam them open with some chopped shallot, parsley stems, bay leaf, crushed garlic, and white wine. Strain, saving the juices, and let cool. Remove the clams from their shells. (East Coast steamers require removing the tough neck from the rest of the clam meat.) Let them soak in their own juice. Cut the carrots, celery, onion, and 2 shallots into a finely diced mirepoix. Finely chop the parsley leaves.

SAUTÉ THE MIREPOIX in butter until cooked but still crunchy. Add the cream and clam juice (let it settle, then pour off the juice carefully, leaving the sand in the bottom of the bowl). Be careful of the salt level when adding the juice. Cook the linguine, and add to the vegetables along with the clams and parsley. Mix all together and serve garnished with ground black pepper.

Variation: This sauce of cream, herbs, and mirepoix is delicious with all kinds of shellfish: mussels, crawfish, clams, shrimp, or any combination. It is especially complementary to lobster with an addition of a little black truffle.

CRAWFISH BISQUE SAUCE & LINGUINE

2 carrots
1 onion
2 stalks celery
4 or 5 cloves garlic
4 tomatoes
Bouquet garni
  (parsley, basil, thyme,
  tarragon, bay leaf)
1 dozen live large crawfish
2 to 3 tablespoons olive oil
Salt, pepper, and cayenne

Cognac
¾ cup dry white wine
½ cup heavy cream
4 cups water
1 tablespoon sweet butter
1 tablespoon chopped
  fresh parsley and tarragon
Lemon
Linguine for 4
Fresh chives

Serves 4

MAKE A MIREPOIX by finely dicing equal quantities of the carrots, onion, and celery, to make a total of 1 cup. Chop the remainder of the vegetables to use for the sauce. Peel and chop the garlic. Core the tomatoes and dice them. Wrap a few stems each of parsley, basil, thyme, and tarragon, and a bay leaf in cheesecloth and tie it with a string to make a bouquet garni.

Rinse the crawfish and sauté them in very hot olive oil. Season with salt, black pepper, and a little cayenne pepper. Cook, stirring frequently, for 4 to 5 minutes. Flame the crawfish with a dash of Cognac, then add the white wine. Continue cooking over a high flame until the wine is reduced by half, then remove from the heat. When the crawfish are cool enough to handle, pull off the tails and shell them. Cover the tails with the cream and chill them.

Crack and pound all of the shells and claws and return them to the pot with the extra vegetables and garlic. Sauté them together for a few minutes, then add the tomatoes, bouquet garni, and water. Bring the sauce to a boil and adjust it to a gentle simmer.

COOK THE SAUCE, skimming occasionally, for 1 to 1½ hours. Strain the sauce through a sieve, using a wooden spoon to press all of the liquid from the shells and vegetables. Return the sauce to the stove and reduce it to 1½ cups.

Cook the mirepoix in a little butter for 5 minutes or so. Season it with salt and pepper and a tablespoon of chopped parsley and tarragon. Add the reduced sauce, the cream, and crawfish tails. Taste for seasoning and add a good squeeze of lemon. Cook the linguine, and add it to the sauce. Mix well and serve garnished with tiny chives.

Variations: Substitute lobster or shrimp or a combination of shellfish in place of the crawfish. – For a deeper-flavored and more complex sauce, use fish fumet instead of water, and when the sauce is cooked, put the shells and vegetables in a blender in small batches, and pulverize them. Then strain through a coarse strainer and again through a fine strainer.

TOMATOES, ANCHOVY, CREAM, & WHOLE-WHEAT PAPPARDELLE

6 salt-packed anchovies
4 cloves garlic
3 large ripe tomatoes
A few sprigs fresh Italian parsley
2 tablespoons olive oil
1 cup heavy cream
Whole-wheat pappardelle for 4

Serves 4

FILET AND RINSE the anchovies. Cut them crosswise in thin little slices. Peel and chop the garlic. Peel and seed 3 large tomatoes, or enough to make approximately 1 cup when roughly chopped. Mince the Italian parsley.

COOK THE GARLIC and half the anchovies in olive oil over a low flame for a minute or two. Add the cream, raise the heat, and season with pepper. When the cream begins to boil, add the tomatoes. Simmer for 2 or 3 minutes, then add the rest of the anchovies. Boil the noodles and add to the sauce. Mix the pasta and the sauce and serve garnished with more black pepper and a generous sprinkling of parsley.

GRILLED TOMATO SAUCE &
WHOLE-WHEAT PASTA

4 large ripe tomatoes
Virgin olive oil
Salt and pepper
Sprigs of fresh marjoram, preferably with flowers
2 or 3 sweet red torpedo onions
2 or 3 cloves garlic
Whole-wheat taglierini for 4

Serves 4

HALVE THE TOMATOES and remove the seeds. Brush them with olive oil, season with salt and pepper, and fill the pockets with fresh marjoram leaves and flowers. Charcoal grill the tomatoes, about 4 to 5 minutes on each side, over a medium-hot fire. The skins will brown and have a tantalizing roasted smell. Slice the red onions into ¼-inch rounds. Brush them with oil and season with salt and pepper. Grill the onions, turning a few times, until they are browned and tender. Roughly chop the tomatoes and cook them, together with the onions, in some olive oil with a little chopped garlic. Simmer just a few minutes while you cook the pasta. Serve the sauce over the taglierini. This pasta is terrific served with grilled lamb or veal chops.

Variations: Sauté leeks and garlic in olive oil. Add some peeled, seeded, and chopped tomatoes and a mixture of chopped fresh herbs: marjoram, basil, thyme, parsley, and so on. Cook the tomatoes just a few minutes and serve over hot pasta. – Pound a few anchovy filets to a smooth paste in a mortar with some garlic and olive oil. Sauté a thinly sliced red onion in olive oil. Add some peeled, seeded, and chopped tomatoes, a pinch of crushed red pepper, black pepper, and the anchovy paste. Cook for a few minutes, then add some pitted black olives, chopped basil, and capers.

101

Spaghetti & Meatballs

Meatballs:
4 cloves garlic
2 shallots
Olive oil
A handful fresh flat-leaf parsley
2 to 3 sprigs fresh thyme
2 slices dry bread
Milk
½ pound ground pork
½ pound ground beef
¼ pound grated Parmesan
Salt and pepper

Sauce:
14 to 16 ripe tomatoes
2 onions
2 or 3 cloves garlic
2 tablespoons virgin olive oil
2 tablespoons tomato paste
A few sprigs fresh oregano with flowers
A few sprigs fresh basil
Salt and pepper
A pinch of crushed red pepper
Prosciutto bone

Spaghetti, fresh or dried, for 4
Fresh parsley
Parmesan

Serves 4

PEEL AND CHOP the garlic and shallots and cook them briefly in a little olive oil. Chop the parsley and thyme together. Soak 2 slices of dry bread, crusts removed, in a little milk until they are moist again. Squeeze out the excess milk and break up the bread. Combine the pork and beef, garlic, shallots, herbs, bread crumbs, and ½ cup Parmesan. Season with salt and pepper. Fry a little bit of the mixture to taste for salt. Form the meatballs. The recipe will make about a dozen and a half that are 1½ inches in diameter. Brown the meatballs in a skillet in a little olive oil. They need only brown on the outside, not cook all the way through. They will finish cooking in the sauce.

PEEL AND SEED the tomatoes and roughly chop them. Finely dice the onion and chop the garlic. Sauté the onion and garlic in 2 tablespoons olive oil. When they have softened, add the tomatoes and tomato paste. Pluck the oregano flowers, cut the basil into thin ribbons, and add them to the sauce. Season with salt and pepper and a pinch of crushed red pepper. Simmer the sauce with a small section of prosciutto bone for 15 minutes. Put the meatballs in the sauce and simmer another 15 or 20 minutes, stirring occasionally. Cook the spaghetti and serve sauced with the tomatoes and meatballs. Garnish with freshly chopped Italian parsley and freshly grated Parmesan.

Variation: Completely cook the sauce and meatball recipe, then remove the meatballs from the sauce and mash them with ⅓ pound fresh ricotta. Stuff this mixture into large parboiled rigatoni, make a single layer of them in a large pan, and cover with the sauce. Garnish the top with freshly grated Parmesan and bake 30 minutes.

BARBECUED ARTICHOKES
& BROKEN GARLIC PASTA

18 small artichokes
Lemon
¾ cup virgin olive oil
Salt and pepper
6 heads small fresh red garlic
6 slices bacon
A handful fresh Italian parsley
½ cup grated dry jack cheese
Taglierini for 4

Serves 4

TRIM THE ARTICHOKES: cut off the tops of the leaves and cut the stalks to the very base of the choke. Pull off the outer leaves, leaving only the tender pale green inner leaves. Cut them in half lengthwise and rub them all over with a juicy lemon. When they are all trimmed, toss with ¼ cup olive oil and marinate for an hour or two. Then season the artichokes with salt and pepper and grill them over a medium-hot charcoal fire. Cook them 10 to 15 minutes, turning frequently, so that they are browned and tender but still a little crunchy. Separate the cloves of garlic. Use the side of a chef's knife to gently flatten the cloves. Slip off the skin. Cut the slices of bacon in small pieces. Chop the parsley leaves and grate the cheese.

FRY THE WHOLE CLOVES of garlic in ½ cup olive oil over very low heat. Stir almost constantly for 15 to 20 minutes while they soften and caramelize. They must not cook over too hot a flame or they will have that burned garlic taste. Fry the bacon pieces separately, then add to the garlic. Add the artichokes, heat thoroughly, and season with ground black pepper. Cook the pasta, and add to the garlic and artichokes. Add the parsley and toss everything together. Serve the pasta and pass around grated dry jack cheese at the table.

ARTICHOKE HEARTS, PROSCIUTTO, & FETTUCCINE

1½ pounds small artichokes	1 cup fresh bread crumbs
Lemon	10 to 12 tablespoons
1 onion	virgin olive oil
3 cloves garlic	Salt and pepper
A handful fresh parsley leaves	Fettuccine for 4
A handful fresh basil leaves	Parmesan
¼ pound thinly sliced	
prosciutto	

Serves 4

PREPARE THE ARTICHOKES by first cutting off the top third of the leaves. Pull off the tough outer leaves, exposing the tender center. Pare around the bottom with a small knife, removing the dark green base of the leaves. Cut the bottoms into quarters and put into water acidulated with lemon. These small artichokes are immature enough that the chokes have not yet developed, so all but the exterior is edible. Dice the onion. Peel and chop the garlic. Chop the parsley and basil. Cut the prosciutto into narrow strips. Toast 1 cup of fresh bread crumbs in the oven until dry and lightly browned, then toss them with a few tablespoons olive oil.

SOFTEN THE ONIONS and garlic in 3 or 4 tablespoons olive oil. Add the artichokes, season with salt and pepper, cover, and braise slowly until tender (approximately 15 to 20 minutes). Add the parsley, basil, prosciutto, and another 4 tablespoons olive oil. Cook the fettuccine and toss with the artichoke mixture. Season with black pepper. Serve garnished with the toasted bread crumbs and freshly grated Parmesan cheese.

OYSTER TORTELLI

16 to 18 oysters
3 shallots
1 sprig fresh thyme
Several sprigs fresh parsley
1-egg pasta dough
2 tablespoons sweet butter
½ cup heavy cream
Pepper

Serves 4

THESE TORTELLI are extremely fragile because of the wetness of the oysters. They must be made and then cooked right away. If they are allowed to sit, the pasta surrounding the oyster will become soggy.

Shuck the oysters and save the juices. Peel and thinly slice the shallots. Pull the leaves from the sprig of thyme and finely chop the parsley.

Roll the pasta very thin, and with a special tortelli cutter or a cookie cutter, cut a round piece of dough for each oyster. Drain the oysters, pat them dry, and place each one on a round of dough. Use your fingertip to moisten the edges with a little oyster juice. Fold the dough over the oyster and press the edges together to make half moons.

SAUTÉ THE SHALLOTS and thyme leaves very gently in the butter until they are soft. Add 4 or 5 tablespoons of oyster juice (according to how salty it is) and the cream. Cook the tortelli and put them in warm bowls. Spoon the sauce over them and garnish with freshly ground black pepper and chopped parsley.

Oysters, Leeks, Pancetta, & Linguine

50 to 60 Olympia oysters
4 leeks
4 very thin slices pancetta
A few sprigs fresh thyme
A few sprigs fresh parsley
2 to 3 tablespoons sweet butter
¾ cup chicken stock
½ cup heavy cream
Linguine for 2
Pepper

Serves 2

OLYMPIA OYSTERS are tiny and delicate. They have a sweet buttery flavor and are not too salty. They are very easy to open and it takes no time at all to do 50 or 60.

Open the oysters, collecting the juice, and set aside. Cut the white part of the leeks into halves. Wash well and cut into long narrow strips. Unroll the pancetta slices and cut into small sections. Take the thyme leaves off the stems. Chop the parsley.

SAUTÉ THE LEEKS in the butter a few minutes. Add the stock and thyme and cook together until the leeks are tender. In the meantime, in another pan, sauté the pancetta until crisp. Remove it from the fat and have ready to add to the noodles. Add the cream, parsley, oysters, and oyster juice to the leeks. Cook the noodles. (The oysters and linguine take about the same amount of time to cook – a minute or so.) Add the pasta and pancetta. Mix well and serve garnished with ground black pepper.

SALMON ROE, SMOKED SALMON, & PASTA SALAD

1 pound ditali or penne
  (small macaroni)
½ cup virgin olive oil
¾ pound tiny green beans
3 green onions
4 thin slices smoked salmon
1 bunch fresh coriander
1 bunch watercress

1 dozen quail eggs
2 limes
Mustard
Lemon zest
Salt and pepper
Niçoise olives
8 ounces salmon roe

Serves 8 to 10

BOIL THE PASTA, drain it, and toss in some of the olive oil. Top and tail the green beans, blanch in boiling salted water, and drain. Thinly slice the green onions. Cut the salmon into thin strips. Pluck the leaves of half the coriander and half the watercress and chop them. Hard cook, then slice, the quail eggs. Mix everything together except the eggs and add the olive oil, the juice of 2 limes, a little mustard, lemon zest, salt and pepper, and some Niçoise olives. Stir in the salmon roe, then taste and correct the seasoning and chill. Garnish the salad with the remaining sprigs of watercress and coriander and sliced quail eggs.

Variation: Cure the fish or shellfish (halibut, scallops, shrimp, etc.) with lime juice and salt and pepper as for seviche. Add fresh vegetables such as multicolored sweet and hot peppers, or cucumbers, or radishes, and so on. Toss with pasta and dress with olive oil and fresh herbs.

TAGLIERINI & GARDEN LETTUCE VINAIGRETTE

2 heads curly endive	Salt and pepper
2 handfuls garden lettuces such as rocket, Bibb, red leaf, etc.	1 clove garlic
	1 salt-packed anchovy filet
2 shallots	Virgin olive oil
Red wine vinegar	Whole-wheat taglierini for 4
Balsamic vinegar	Pitted black olives

Serves 4

SELECT ONLY the choice lettuce leaves and carefully wash and dry them. Keep the curly endive separate from the tender garden lettuces. Make the vinaigrette. Finely dice 2 shallots and soak them in approximately ¼ cup of vinegar (a blend of vinegars is nice for an interesting balance of flavor and acid). Season with salt and pepper. Add a crushed garlic clove (to be removed later), a rinsed and finely chopped anchovy filet, and approximately ½ to ¾ cup olive oil. The exact amounts of vinegar, oil, and salt are a matter of personal taste.

SAUTÉ THE CURLY ENDIVE with about one-third of the vinaigrette over a gentle flame until just wilted. Cook the taglierini. Turn off the fire under the endive and add the rest of the vinaigrette, the garden lettuces, and the pasta. Toss all together, taste for salt and pepper, and correct the seasoning. Serve warm, garnished with a sprinkling of pitted black olives.

Variations: Any number of combinations of greens are delicious cooked this way: mustard, chard, sorrel, lamb's lettuce, purslane, dandelion, and so on. Bear in mind the respective cooking times of strong and delicate greens. – For very tender garden salad do not cook the greens at all but toss them with warm vinaigrette and hot pasta and they will wilt from the heat of the noodles. Garnish with strips of anchovy filet and dried tomato. This also makes an excellent cold pasta.

WILD MUSHROOMS, PINE NUTS, CHICKEN, & TAGLIATELLE

½ ounce dried *Boletus edulis* mushrooms
1 cup reduced chicken stock
4 chicken breasts
2 to 3 tablespoons light olive oil
A few sprigs fresh thyme

Fresh chives
6 green onions
1 large clove garlic
¼ cup toasted pine nuts
A few sprigs fresh parsley
Salt and pepper
Tagliatelle for 4

Serves 4

SOAK THE MUSHROOMS in hot water. When they are soft, look them over carefully to make sure there are no pockets of dirt, and slice them thin. Save the juice, and depending on the strength of flavor, add a few tablespoons to the chicken stock. Bone and trim the chicken breasts, then cut, crossgrain, into thin strips. Marinate the slices in a little olive oil and some chopped thyme leaves and chives. Cut the green onions into a julienne and chop the garlic. Lightly toast the pine nuts. Chop the parsley.

SAUTÉ THE MUSHROOMS in a little olive oil for 3 or 4 minutes. Season the mushrooms with salt and pepper. Reduce the heat and add the garlic and parsley. Cook another 1 to 2 minutes and then add the hot chicken stock. In a separate pan (a large sauté pan or a wok), sauté the chicken. Cook the chicken very hot and fast, about 1 minute, so that the outside browns and inside stays pink and moist. Cook the pasta and then add to the mushrooms along with the green onions, chicken, and pine nuts. Toss together, taste for seasoning, and serve.

Variation: Use fresh boletes or other fresh wild mushrooms in place of the dried ones.

PAPPARDELLE & FRIED EGGPLANT

1 large eggplant
Light olive oil
Red wine vinegar
Salt and pepper
A handful fresh basil leaves
3 salt-packed anchovies
2 cloves garlic
2 handfuls young rocket leaves
Semolina pappardelle for 4

Serves 4

CUT THE EGGPLANT in half lengthwise and then cut it into approximately ¼-inch slices. Fry these slices one layer at a time in very hot olive oil until nicely browned on both sides. Remove them and drain on paper towels. When they are all cooked, cut the slices in halves or thirds. Put them on a platter and sprinkle with vinegar. Season with salt and pepper and mix with the basil, chopped. Let the eggplant marinate for an hour or more. Filet, rinse, and chop the anchovies. Peel and chop the garlic. Wash and dry the rocket leaves.

HEAT THE GARLIC and anchovies very gently in a few tablespoons olive oil. Add the eggplant. Cook the pasta and add to the pan. Season with black pepper, and at the last moment add the rocket leaves. Toss all together and serve.

Variations: Instead of rocket add whole basil leaves. – The eggplant is also delicious with young garlic cloves fried in their skins with marjoram as the main herb instead of basil and rocket. – Cut Japanese eggplant and zucchini into julienne. Fry them in olive oil with garlic and salt and pepper. Toss with pasta and garnish with freshly grated Parmesan and chopped herbs.

111

Duck Liver, Green Bean, & Walnut Pasta

4 duck livers	1 tablespoon walnut oil
4 shallots	Salt and pepper
¼ cup walnut halves	Sherry vinegar
⅓ pound tiny green beans	1 tablespoon virgin olive oil
2 sprigs fresh thyme	½ cup reduced squab or
A small handful fresh	duck stock
Italian parsley	Tagliatelle for 2

Serves 2

TRIM THE DUCK LIVERS. Cut away the connective tissue between the lobes. Peel and thinly slice the shallots. Chop the walnut halves into 2 or 3 pieces and lightly toast in the oven. Top and tail the green beans. Pull the leaves from the sprigs of fresh thyme. Finely chop the parsley leaves.

IN A LARGE SAUTÉ PAN, fry the duck livers in a tablespoon of hot walnut oil. Season with salt and pepper and add the thyme leaves. Cooking approximately 2 minutes on each side, fry them hot, so that they get a little brown and crispy on the outside. Test them for doneness with a touch of your finger. They should be a little soft at the center and give a bit so that they will have a pink and juicy interior. At the last moment, add a splash of sherry vinegar, approximately 1 tablespoon, and remove from the heat. Remove the livers from the pan to a plate and return the pan to the stove. Add the shallots and olive oil and cook over low heat. Blanch the beans a minute or two in the boiling pasta water. While they are cooking, heat the stock in a small saucepan and slice the livers. Remove the beans from the water, drain, and add them to the shallots. Add the warm stock to the beans and bring to a simmer. Cook the pasta, and add to the beans, along with the livers and the walnuts. Toss everything together, season with salt and pepper. Taste for vinegar, and correct if necessary. Serve garnished with chopped parsley.

Variations: Use fresh rabbit liver in place of duck liver. – Sauté squab, duck, or rabbit liver in butter and oil with chanterelles and chopped shallots. At the end add a bit of port and brandy. Purée the livers and mushrooms, add a little cream and butter, and correct the seasoning. Fill the ravioli, following the directions on page 12, and serve in a cream sauce or clear soup garnished with herbs.

Dried Tomatoes, Green Beans, & Tagliatelle

12 ounces tiny green beans (2 large handfuls)
10 or 12 sun-dried tomatoes
4 cloves garlic
2 sprigs fresh savory
Small bunch fresh Italian parsley
6 to 8 tablespoons virgin olive oil
Salt and pepper
Tagliatelle for 4
Parmesan

Serves 4

PINCH OFF THE TOPS and ends of the beans. Cut the dried tomatoes into a julienne. Peel and finely chop the garlic. Pull the leaves from the savory sprigs and mince them. Chop the parsley.

Heat the olive oil, add the savory and garlic, and cook very gently 1 or 2 minutes. Be careful not to let the garlic brown. Blanch the beans for about 1 minute in the salted boiling pasta water. Remove and add them, along with the dried tomatoes, to the garlic and oil. Season with salt and pepper. Cook the tagliatelle and add to the vegetables. Toss all together and lightly season again. Serve garnished with the parsley and freshly grated Parmesan.

Variation: Gently fry some chopped garlic in a lot of olive oil. Add thinly sliced Japanese eggplant and fry until golden. Boil and add fettuccine and season with salt and pepper. Add julienned dried tomato, chopped parsley, a little more chopped raw garlic, and freshly grated Parmesan. Toss together and serve.

WHITE TRUFFLE PASTA

Fresh white truffle
Heavy cream
Salt and pepper
Thin fettuccine

HEAT THE CREAM and reduce it slightly. Cook the fettuccine and
add it to the cream. Season with salt and pepper. Serve on hot dishes
and shave thin slices of truffle all over the top.

Variation: Staggs Pasta – Cook very fine fettuccine made with extra
egg yolk in the dough. Toss the noodles in fresh sweet butter, season
with salt and coarsely ground black pepper, and serve with shaved
truffle all over the top.

WINTER
PASTA

Martine labro-

A winter larder filled with preserves of all kinds (a crock of duck confit, jars of dried tomatoes and pickled onions, sacks of dried beans, *pissala*, and home-cured olives), hams and sausages curing in the rafters over the chimney, and a root cellar filled with winter vegetables – even though most of us don't have all these, cooking as if we did suits winter appetites. Good cooking in winter, even in mild climates, requires more planning than at other times of the year.

Since winter food is more concocted than other seasonal food, flavors are deeper and more complex, and dishes often require careful preparation and long slow cooking. It's the season of stews simmered patiently on the back of the stove, gratins baked in earthenware dishes, pasta dishes like braised duck with buckwheat noodles, or semolina noodles with sausage and winter greens. There are some fresh foods in winter to provide relief. Many shellfish are at their best in winter, oysters in particular. And depending on the climate, you can enjoy your own winter greens and lettuces for most of the season, if they are protected from frost in hot beds or even grown indoors.

I think of pasta more often as a first course than as the major dish of a winter menu. A simple menu might begin with onion confit and winter green pasta, continue with a grilled guinea hen, and end with prune and Armagnac ice cream. A similar meal could start with chard, goat cheese, and buckwheat pasta, followed with a loin of lamb sautéed in walnut oil and finish with homemade spumoni ice cream. Among the substantial pasta dishes in this chapter, wild mushroom lasagne would be especially good as a main course flanked by a beet and lamb's-lettuce salad and a persimmon pudding. And as the only course of a festive midnight supper, what could be better than buckwheat noodles with crème fraîche and caviar, served with Champagne? Possibly plain buttered pasta loaded with black truffles . . .

There are recipes here that are cooked in red wine and should be served with more of the same – pasta with Barolo and duck gizzard sauce and rabbit stewed in red wine. Generally these dishes are well matched with aged full-bodied wines that are full of character (Piedmontese wines, Bordeaux, Burgundies). This is by far the best time of year to get out your favorite, oldest bottles.

ONION CONFIT & WINTER GREENS PASTA

Onion Confit:
4 onions
4 tablespoons sweet butter
Salt and pepper
1 tablespoon sugar
A few sprigs fresh thyme
2 cups red wine
¼ cup red wine vinegar
¼ cup sherry or tarragon vinegar
Cassis (optional)

1 cup chicken stock
2 bunches winter greens
   (chard, turnip, mustard, etc.)
Salt and pepper
4 tablespoons sweet butter
Fettuccine for 4

Serves 4

THE CONFIT can be prepared long in advance. In fact, this is about twice as much as is needed for 4 servings of pasta, but it does not cook well in smaller quantities. It keeps quite well for about a week and can be used for hors d'oeuvre croutons, sandwiches, and pizzas.

Slice the onions very thin. Brown the butter in a large pot and add the onions. Season with salt and pepper. Cover and cook for 5 minutes or so, until the onions begin to soften and release their juices. Sprinkle with a tablespoon of sugar and cook, covered, another few minutes, allowing the sugar to caramelize slightly. Then add the leaves of a few sprigs of thyme, the red wine, red wine vinegar, and the ¼ cup sherry or tarragon vinegar. A tablespoon of cassis (black currant liqueur), if you have it, is a nice addition. Lower the heat to a slow simmer and cook approximately 1 to 1½ hours, until the liquid is all but gone and what remains is of a syrupy texture.

THIS PASTA is a perfect accompaniment to roast or grilled chicken or squab. In a large sauté pan, reduce the chicken stock gently. Wash the greens. Trim away the large stems and cut the leaves in wide strips. Blanch them in the pasta water for 1 minute or so, then add them to the stock. Season with salt and pepper. Add the butter. Cook the fettuccine and add to the greens along with approximately half the onion confit recipe. Mix all together and serve.

Variation: A spring version of this recipe can be made with fresh small whole onions, cooked in the wine in the same way, and a mixture of spring garden greens.

SAUSAGE, WINTER GREENS, & SEMOLINA PASTA

2 leeks
3 cloves garlic
2 bunches winter greens
  (mustard, beet, turnip,
  red chard, etc.)
4 sausages (sweet Italian,
  or spicy, or hot, etc.)

6 to 7 tablespoons virgin olive oil
Semolina linguine for 4
Salt and pepper
Pitted black olives
Crushed red pepper (optional)
Parmesan

Serves 4

WASH AND THINLY SLICE the leeks. Peel and chop the garlic. Remove any large stems from the greens, cut the leaves crosswise into a chiffonade, and wash and dry them. Slice the sausages.

STEW THE LEEKS, garlic, and sausage in about 5 tablespoons olive oil for 10 minutes or so. Add the greens and continue cooking for 5 minutes more, until they are soft and wilted. The addition of a little water or stock will help to steam them. Moisten the mixture with another tablespoon or two of olive oil. Cook the pasta and add it to the pan. Toss all together and taste for seasoning. Serve garnished with a generous sprinkling of pitted black olives and a little crushed red pepper if you like it spicy. Serve freshly grated Parmesan cheese at the table.

CHARD, GOAT CHEESE, & BUCKWHEAT PASTA

2 cloves garlic
1 large bunch red chard
2 tablespoons sweet butter
Salt and pepper
1 cup heavy cream
2 ounces Sonoma goat cheese
Buckwheat pappardelle for 3

Serves 3

CHOP THE GARLIC FINE. Stem the chard. Cut the leaves crosswise in ribbons and wash them. Blanch the leaves in boiling salted water for half a minute. Remove from the water and drain. Stew the chard gently in the butter with the garlic for 4 to 5 minutes. Season with salt and pepper.

HEAT THE CREAM. Crumble the goat cheese, add half of it to the cream, and whisk until very smooth. Add the chard and simmer gently. Cook the pasta and add to the chard along with the rest of the goat cheese. Mix well and serve garnished with black pepper.

Ravioli with Chicken, Ricotta, & Greens

1 bunch turnip greens
1 bunch Swiss chard
1 onion
4 cloves garlic
¼ pound pancetta, sliced thin
A handful fresh basil leaves
2 chicken legs
2 cups chicken stock

3 tablespoons olive oil
¼ pound fresh ricotta
3 tablespoons olive paste
Salt and pepper
3-egg pasta dough
  yield: 70 to 80 two-inch ravioli
4 tablespoons sweet butter

Serves 6

PULL THE STEMS from the turnip leaves. Discard any that are too old or overgrown. Do the same for the chard leaves. It is easier to cut the stalk from the chard with a paring knife. Make stacks of the leaves and cut them crosswise into fine ribbons. Wash and spin them dry. Finely dice the onion. Mince the garlic. Unroll the slices of pancetta and cut them into small pieces. Cut the basil leaves in thin ribbons, saving some leaves to cut just at the end for a garnish. Poach the chicken legs in the stock until just cooked, a little on the rare side. Set aside until cool. Strain the stock and reduce it a little to concentrate the flavor.

Heat the olive oil in a large pot and cook the onion, garlic, and pancetta until they soften. Add the greens and basil and stew slowly until they are quite tender. Remove the chicken meat from the bone and cut into fine pieces. When the greens are cooked, remove from the fire and let them cool. Combine the chicken, greens, basil chiffonade, ricotta, and olive paste. Taste for salt and season with black pepper.

Roll the pasta and fill the ravioli in the usual way (see page 12). Boil them in salted water and then remove to the pan of simmering chicken stock. Add the butter. Serve the ravioli with the broth and garnish with a fine chiffonade of the remaining basil.

Variations: Start with one to one proportions of Gorgonzola and fresh ricotta. If the Gorgonzola is well aged and very strong flavored, more ricotta will be needed. Mix the cheeses and taste to determine the right balance. Season with ground black pepper and add a fine chiffonade of basil leaves. Fill and cook the ravioli in the usual way and serve with cream warmed with more basil chiffonade. – Make a filling of equal quantities of Sonoma goat cheese and fresh mozzarella. Add some prosciutto sliced thin and then chopped. Finely chop some garlic, soften it in a little butter and add to the cheese. Season with black pepper and some finely chopped marjoram and thyme. Roll the pasta and fill the ravioli. Serve sauced with warm cream garnished with black pepper and chives. – Cook spinach leaves in butter with onions, garlic, salt, pepper, and nutmeg. Purée and mix with ricotta pecorino cheese, a little cream, and egg. Fill the ravioli and serve in butter with chopped sage.

SMASHED POTATO RAVIOLI

1 pound potatoes
Bouquet garni
  (1 head garlic, black peppercorns,
  parsley stems, fresh thyme)
3 to 4 tablespoons sweet butter
1½ to 2 cups heavy cream
Salt and pepper
2-egg pasta dough
  yield: 40 to 50 two-inch ravioli
Fresh chives

Serves 4

THIS COMBINATION of starches sounds quite indelicate but the ravioli are really just the opposite. They are especially good garnished with a very dry French goat cheese, finely grated.

A mixture of several varieties of potatoes makes the best textured purée. Peel and boil the potatoes with the bouquet garni. When they are soft, remove the bouquet and put the potatoes through a food mill. Beat in some butter and a little cream to make a smooth rich purée. Season with salt and pepper. Roll the pasta and fill the ravioli (a pastry bag works well) with the potato purée (see page 12). Boil the ravioli gently in salted water, and serve in a sauce of the remaining warmed cream, garnished with black pepper and chives.

Variations: Serve the ravioli in a sauce of fresh sorrel leaves melted in cream. – Include a slice of fresh black truffle in each ravioli. – Make pasta flavored with chopped sage and fill the ravioli with a mixture of puréed potatoes, stewed leeks and garlic, and fontina cheese. – To make artichoke heart ravioli: trim large artichokes down to the heart. Slice and stew them slowly in a mixture of butter and olive oil with chopped shallot, chervil, thyme, and salt and pepper until very tender. Purée the mixture, correct the seasoning, and add a tablespoon of chopped chervil and parsley. – To make winter squash ravioli: cut the squash (acorn, butternut, Golden Nugget, etc.) in half, remove the seeds, season the inside with salt, pepper, a sprig of thyme, some unpeeled garlic cloves, and drizzle with a little olive oil. Place cut side down on a baking sheet and bake until very soft. Remove the pulp and pass through a food mill. Correct the seasoning and add a little butter or cream to soften the purée. – Ravioli filled with different vegetable

128

purées are delicious served together with roast chicken. Make a sauce from the pan juices, Marsala, cream, and chicken stock and serve with the ravioli. – Try other vegetable purées – fava bean, turnip, celery root, beet and onion, peas and spinach, pumpkin . . .

GRILLED DUCK LIVERS &
MUSTARD HERB BUTTER PASTA

¼ pound duck livers
Olive oil
1 shallot
1 small clove garlic
4 tablespoons sweet butter
1 teaspoon Dijon mustard
1 tablespoon chopped combined
  fresh thyme, marjoram, chervil,
  and sage

1 tablespoon chopped
  fresh parsley
1 tablespoon fresh chives
Salt and pepper
Lemon juice
Black pepper fettuccine for 2

Serves 2

WASH THE LIVERS and towel-dry them. Cut away the connective tissue between the lobes. Skewer them on brochettes and marinate in a little olive oil. Finely chop the shallot and garlic and mix well with the butter and mustard and all of the herbs. Season with salt, pepper, and lemon juice.

SALT AND PEPPER the liver brochettes and grill them over a hot charcoal fire, about 2 minutes on each side. They should still be pink and juicy at the center. When they are nearly done, cook the pasta. Melt the mustard herb butter and add the cooked and drained noodles. Toss well to coat the pasta with the butter, and serve the noodles as a nest for the grilled livers.

Variation: The mustard herb butter is a versatile sauce with other innards grilled or fried: sweetbreads, kidneys, hearts, chicken livers, rabbit livers, and so on.

BUCKWHEAT NOODLES & BRAISED DUCK

A 4 to 5 pound duck
3 star anise
½ teaspoon black peppercorns
Salt
1 onion
A few sprigs fresh parsley
4 cloves garlic
2 bay leaves

Duck stock
1½ heads radicchio
6 green onions
¼ pound Niçoise olives
1 cup dry bread crumbs
2 tablespoons olive oil
Buckwheat fettuccine for 4

Serves 4

THE DUCK is cooked somewhat in the Chinese style. First remove the head, neck, wing tips, and feet of the duck and save for stock. Pound some star anise and black pepper together in a mortar with a pestle. Rub the powder all over the outside of the duck. Season inside and out with salt. Stuff the cavity with some chopped onion, parsley, garlic, bay leaves, and any other fresh herbs you might have. Put in a roasting pan on a bed of onions and cook in a 400°F oven for 15 minutes. Remove from the oven and baste with the rendered fat in the pan. Add a little water to the pan. Cover with foil and return to a 350°F oven. Cook for another hour or so until quite tender and juicy. Let the duck cool, then remove all of the meat from the bones. Remove the skin from the meat and reserve. Cut the meat into narrow strips. Pour the juices from the carcass over the meat and set aside.

Take all of the bones plus the head, wings, and feet and make a stock (see page 184). Reduce the stock to approximately 1½ cups. Cut the radicchio crosswise into thin ribbons and the green onions into a julienne. Pit and chop the black olives. Peel and chop the garlic. Cut the duck skin into small pieces.

Fry the duck skin until it is brown and crisp. Add the dry bread crumbs and keep cooking gently while you sauté the radicchio with the garlic in a small amount of olive oil until it begins to wilt. Season the radicchio with salt and pepper. Add the green onions, olives, duck meat, and warm duck stock. Cook the noodles and add to the pan. Mix well and taste for salt and pepper. Serve garnished with the crisp skin and bread crumb mixture.

Variation: Substitute red cabbage, cut into very fine chiffonade and blanched a moment in boiling water before frying. Or use Belgian endive instead of radicchio.

131

Barolo & Duck Gizzard Sauce with Pappardelle

1½ pounds duck gizzards
2 carrots
2 stalks celery
2 onions
3 or 4 cloves garlic
2 sprigs fresh thyme
1 sprig fresh marjoram
A handful fresh parsley leaves
6 to 8 tablespoons sweet butter

2 tablespoons olive oil
1 bay leaf
Salt and pepper
¾ bottle Barolo wine
Approximately 3 cups bird stock
  (duck, chicken, pigeon)
Pappardelle for 6
Parmesan

Serves 6

TRIM OFF the membrane surrounding and connecting the gizzards. Cut the carrots, celery, and onions into a fine mirepoix. Peel and chop the garlic. Take the leaves from the sprigs of fresh thyme, a sprig of marjoram, and chop them together with the parsley leaves, reserving some parsley for garnish.

START THE MIREPOIX cooking in a pot with approximately 2 tablespoons each butter and olive oil, add the garlic and herbs, and cook until it begins to soften. Add the duck gizzards, season with salt and pepper, and cook gently a few minutes. Add the red wine and bring to a simmer. When the wine is reduced by half, add the stock and continue to simmer very gently. The total cooking time should be about 1½ hours. When the gizzards are cooked they will be tender but not too soft, still retaining a chewy texture. At this point remove just the gizzards from the pot with a slotted spoon. Let them cool slightly. Taste the sauce for seasoning and refresh with a little more garlic and parsley and a good lump of butter. Finely chop the gizzards by hand with a knife. (Unfortunately, a food processor is not suitable for this step. It tends to purée the gizzards and their special texture is lost.) Return them to the sauce and let it all simmer together a little longer. If lacking in liquid, add some more stock.

Cook the pappardelle and toss in butter with salt and pepper. Spoon the sauce over them and garnish with freshly grated Parmesan and chopped parsley.

Variations: Try this sauce in a lasagne. If you have some black truffle, put slices between the layers and it will be heavenly. – This is also a very good way to cook beef tongue. First braise the tongue in simmering water with vegetables and herbs for 45 minutes, then drain, peel, and trim it. Cut the tongue in thick slices and proceed with the recipe, substituting the tongue for gizzards.

FETTUCCINE WITH RABBIT STEWED IN RED WINE

A 2 to 3 pound rabbit
  and its liver
Marinade:
  olive oil, thyme, savory, bay
  leaf, shallots, juniper berries,
  Beaumes-de-Venise wine
3 dozen tiny onions,
  both red and white
8 to 10 cloves garlic
Sprigs of fresh thyme, savory,
  and parsley

1 bay leaf
1 bottle red wine,
  such as St. Joseph or Côte Rôtie
1 quart veal or bird stock
Salt and pepper
Virgin olive oil
Cognac
½ cup heavy cream
Fettuccine for 6
Sweet butter
Fresh chervil leaves

Serves 6

RABBIT STEWED slowly in red wine with sweet onions and herbs is the sauce for this pasta dish.

Separate the rabbit into serving pieces: legs, loin, and ribs. Marinate the pieces overnight with a little olive oil, sprigs of fresh herbs, a few crushed juniper berries, 2 or 3 sliced shallots, and some Beaumes-de-Venise wine. The next day, remove the rabbit from the marinade and start it cooking in a pot with the peeled tiny onions, garlic, some sprigs of herbs, bay leaf, the bottle of red wine, and stock.

SIMMER THE STEW very gently, skimming occasionally, for approximately 2 hours. Remove the rabbit pieces from the sauce and let them cool. The sauce will have reduced by about one-third. Let it cook down a little further, to about half of the original volume. Taste for salt and correct the seasoning. Season the liver with salt and pepper and sauté it in a little olive oil about 2 minutes on each side. Flame with a little Cognac and remove from the fire. Purée the liver in a food processor or blender to a very smooth paste. Bone the rabbit meat and leave it in large pieces. Return the meat to the sauce. Add the liver purée and the cream. Simmer gently and taste again for seasoning.

Cook the pasta, drain, and toss with a little butter, salt, and pepper. Serve the rabbit sauce over the noodles and garnish with fresh chervil.

Variation: This method of slowly stewing the meat in red wine is an excellent way to cook whole squab or duck legs.

WILD MUSHROOM LASAGNE

2 pounds fresh wild
  mushrooms
  (chanterelles, blewits,
  Lepiotas, boletes,
  field mushrooms, etc.)
4 or 5 cloves garlic
A handful fresh parsley leaves
2 or 3 sprigs fresh thyme
½ ounce dried *Boletus edulis*
9 tablespoons sweet butter

3 tablespoons all-purpose flour
1 cup milk
1½ cups half-and-half
Salt and pepper
Nutmeg
½ cup heavy cream
4 tablespoons virgin olive oil
1 cup beef or pigeon stock
2-egg pasta dough
Parmesan

Serves 6

BRUSH OR WIPE the mushrooms clean and thinly slice them. Peel and chop the garlic. Finely chop the parsley and thyme leaves. Soak the dried mushrooms in enough hot water to just cover them.

Make a béchamel sauce: Melt 3 tablespoons butter and whisk the flour into it. Cook gently for 4 to 5 minutes, then let the roux cool a bit. Mix the milk and half-and-half, heat it until almost boiling, then whisk it into the roux. Bring it to a boil and stir frequently to keep the mixture very smooth. Season the béchamel with salt, pepper, and a subtle scraping of nutmeg. Let it simmer very gently for approximately an hour. Pour off ¼ cup or so of the juice from the soaking mushrooms and add it to the sauce. Stir in ½ cup of cream and taste for seasoning. Let the sauce cool while cooking the mushrooms and pasta.

COMBINE THE MUSHROOMS and sauté in four batches with a tablespoon each of butter and olive oil. Season each batch with salt and pepper and cook 4 to 5 minutes until tender and juicy, during the last minute add a little chopped garlic, parsley, and thyme. At the end add approximately ¼ cup stock to each batch and cook it down to a syrupy sauce.

Roll the pasta very thin, cut it to the size of your dish, and cook it according to the instructions on page 12. These quantities will fill a dish 9 by 12 by 2 inches. Line the buttered dish with pasta and spread it with some of the béchamel sauce. Cover the sauce with approximately one-sixth of the mushrooms. Continue layering pasta, sauce,

135

and mushrooms for 5 or 6 more layers. Sprinkle freshly grated Parmesan cheese over the top sheet of pasta and dot it with about 2 tablespoons butter. Cover the dish with foil and bake in a 350°F oven for 20 minutes. Remove the foil and bake another 20 minutes until the top is browned.

WILD MUSHROOM & GREEN PASTA GRATIN

2 ounces dried *Boletus edulis*
3 tablespoons sweet butter
1 tablespoon all-purpose flour
1½ cups reduced chicken stock
1 cup heavy cream
Salt and pepper

Nutmeg
1 clove garlic
Sprigs of fresh parsley
Green fettuccine for 4
Parmesan

Serves 4

THIS PASTA is gratinéed in a hot oven. The top is browned and crusty, the interior creamy and aromatic. The recipe works very well with other species of mushrooms as well, fresh or dried: morels, horn of plenty, and so on.

Put the dried mushrooms in a bowl and cover with boiling water. Let them soak until soft. To make the sauce, melt 1 tablespoon butter in a saucepan. Add the flour and blend together. Let the roux cook gently a few minutes. Whisk in 1½ cups reduced chicken stock and the cream. Season with salt and pepper and a suggestion of nutmeg. Draw off 2 to 3 tablespoons of the juice from the mushrooms and add to the sauce. (How much mushroom liquid is added to the sauce is a matter of taste and the strength of the mushroom flavor. It is better if subtle and not overpowering. There will be more flavor added by the mushrooms themselves in the final stages of cooking.) Put the mixture in the top of a double boiler and simmer for an hour or so. Carefully sort through the mushrooms and cut away any pockets of dirt and grit. These are usually found at the base of the stem. Cut them into small slices. Chop the garlic and parsley.

SAUTÉ THE MUSHROOMS in butter a few minutes. Season with salt and pepper, then add the garlic and parsley. Cook the mushrooms as if they were fresh. Add the sauce. Cook the fettuccine and add to the mushroom sauce. Season the noodles. Put into a buttered gratin dish, or individual dishes. Cover the top with freshly grated Parmesan and put into a hot oven (400° to 425°F) for 15 to 20 minutes for a large dish, less for small dishes. It is ready when the top is crusty and golden.

137

LOBSTER & SCALLOP RAVIOLI

A 1½ pound live lobster
Several sprigs fresh parsley
Lemon
Cayenne
¾ pound scallops
4 or 5 shallots
4 tablespoons sweet butter
A handful fresh basil leaves
Salt and pepper

1 carrot
1 onion
1 celery stalk
1 sprig fresh thyme
1 bay leaf
1 large tomato
2-egg pasta dough
  yield: 40 to 45 two-inch ravioli
½ cup heavy cream

Serves 4

COOK THE LOBSTER in very salty boiling water flavored with a few parsley sprigs, lemon juice, and cayenne for 5 to 6 minutes. Drain the lobster and let it cool. Trim off the tough little muscle on the side of each scallop, then cut the scallops into very small pieces. Peel and finely chop the shallots and melt them in 4 tablespoons butter until soft. Shell the lobster tails and claws and cut into small pieces like the scallops. Save the coral from the head portion of the lobster and add it to the lobster and scallop mixture. Save the shells and scallop trimmings to make a little broth. Cut the basil into a fine chiffonade and add half to the mixture. Combine the shellfish, add the shallots, and season with salt, pepper, and lemon juice.

Make a fumet with the lobster shells, scallop trimmings, and 3 cups of water. Add thinly sliced carrot, onion, and celery stalk, some parsley, the thyme, bay leaf, and chopped tomato. Simmer for 45 minutes or so and strain. Reduce the broth to approximately 1½ cups. Roll the pasta and fill the ravioli (see page 12).

SIMMER THE BROTH and the cream together while cooking the ravioli in gently boiling salted water. When cooked, remove them to the sauce and simmer another minute. Serve with the sauce and garnish with the remaining basil chiffonade.

Variations: Serve the ravioli in different sauces. A lobster bisque type of sauce can be made with the shells; employ a method similar to that for the crawfish bisque sauce on page 98. – Try them with basil butter made with chopped basil, sweet butter, and seasoning. – Or a *fines herbes* butter made with chopped chervil, tarragon, parsley, chives, shallots, and seasoning. – Or a less rich version with just a broth made from the shells without an addition of cream. – Another possibility is a stuffing of lobster meat and a butter made with a purée of roasted red peppers and seasonings.

Salt Cod Ravioli in Fish Broth

¼ pound boneless filet of salt cod
6 or 7 cloves garlic
¼ cup heavy cream
½ cup virgin olive oil
Pepper
Lemon
1 potato (optional)
2-egg pasta dough
2 quarts fish stock
Sprigs of fresh chervil or ripe tomato

Serves 4

THE FRENCH call this creamy, garlicky purée of salt cod *brandade*. The fish is salted and dried to preserve it. Before cooking, it must be soaked in fresh water to reconstitute and de-salt it. Then it is poached and blended to a purée with warm cream, olive oil, and pounded garlic.

Soak the cod for 2 to 3 days in cold water in the refrigerator. Change the water once or twice a day. After the fish is de-salted, poach it in barely simmering water for about 8 minutes, until it is tender but not overcooked. Lift it out of the poaching liquid and flake it while it is still warm. Remove all of the bones and dark spots from the cod.

PEEL THE GARLIC and crush 2 cloves slightly. Heat the crushed cloves over low heat with the cream. Pound the rest of the garlic to a purée in a mortar. Warm the olive oil over low heat. Put about half the oil, all of the cod, and half the pounded garlic in a pan over very low heat, and work the mixture to a rough paste with a pestle or wooden spoon. Put the pan over simmering water and finish the purée by alternately adding the warm cream and olive oil while pounding the mixture to make a rich homogeneous paste. Depending on the texture of the purée, it may or may not require all the cream and oil; it should not be too wet. Season the mixture with more garlic, if necessary, and add black pepper and lemon juice to taste. If the purée is too salty, add enough of a boiled and riced potato to balance the flavor. Let the filling cool to room temperature; it must be firm and dry for the ravioli.

Roll the pasta and fill the ravioli in the usual way (see page 12). Heat the fish stock to a simmer. Cook the ravioli in a large pot of gently boiling water. When they are cooked, remove them with a slotted spoon to warm soup bowls or a tureen and ladle the broth over them. Garnish the dishes with sprigs of fresh chervil or some peeled and seeded tomato.

Variation: Make tortellini instead of ravioli and serve them in a grilled tomato sauce garnished with olives and sautéed red pepper.

141

CAVIAR, CRÈME FRAÎCHE,
& BUCKWHEAT NOODLES

CAVIAR, CRÈME FRAÎCHE, butter, and buckwheat is a divine combination, perfect with Champagne. The rule of thumb with caviar is to purchase as much as possible of the best available that your budget will allow.

Make very thin delicate buckwheat taglierini. Cook the pasta, and toss with melted butter and ground black pepper. For each plate, spoon a few tablespoons of crème fraîche over the noodles and top that with an ounce or two of caviar. This is an exquisite midnight supper.

TRUFFLE, CHANTERELLE, & ENDIVE PASTA

½ to 1 ounce black truffle
1 cup heavy cream
4 Belgian endives
1½ cups reduced chicken stock
6 tablespoons sweet butter
⅓ pound chanterelles
2 shallots
Salt and pepper
Fettuccine for 4

Serves 4

CUT THE TRUFFLE into a fine julienne and marinate it in the cream. Braise the endives with half of the stock and half of the butter, covered, in a 350°F oven. When they are cooked and have cooled, cut them in slices. Clean and slice the chanterelles and dice the shallots.

SAUTÉ THE CHANTERELLES and shallots in the remaining butter and season with salt and pepper. Add the chicken stock and the remaining braising liquid from the endives, and reduce by half. Add the cream, truffles, and endives, and reduce the sauce a bit more. Cook the fettuccine, and add to the sauce. Season with salt and pepper, toss, and serve.

Variation: Cut fresh black truffle into julienne. Rub the inside of a bowl with a crushed garlic clove, and marinate the truffle with a little Cognac in the bowl. When ready to serve the pasta, cook the truffle in cream for a few minutes. Boil fine noodles and add them to the cream, season with salt and pepper, and serve.

PASTA ALFREDO

1 cup heavy cream
2 tablespoons sweet butter
¾ cup freshly grated Parmesan
Pepper
Thin fettuccine for 2

Serves 2

BRING THE CREAM and butter to a boil in a sauté pan. Reduce the heat and simmer for 30 seconds. Add half the Parmesan, a little freshly ground black pepper, whisk until smooth, and remove from the heat. Cook the fettuccine and add to the cream. Add the rest of the Parmesan, toss the noodles well in the sauce, and serve immediately. Garnish with more black pepper.

Variation: Fry pieces of bacon and chopped shallot separately and add to the sauce at the end.

GARLIC, PARSLEY, ANCHOVY, & SPAGHETTI

6 salt-packed anchovies
Several sprigs fresh Italian parsley
5 or 6 cloves garlic
Dried spaghetti or linguine for 4
½ to ¾ cup virgin olive oil
Lemon

Serves 4

THIS IS ONE of those very satisfying pastas that can be made in just a few minutes. It's perfect when you arrive home late and you're ravenous.

Rinse and filet the anchovies. Cut two of them in thin strips and save for a garnish. Finely chop the rest. Mince some Italian parsley to make 4 to 5 tablespoons. Peel and chop the garlic.

START THE PASTA cooking and when it is nearly done, put the oil and garlic in a pan over a low flame. Let the garlic sizzle gently about a minute, but don't let it brown. When the aroma starts to fill the room, remove the pan from the flame, and add the anchovies. Stir them into the garlic oil, then add the pasta and parsley. Toss well and add some coarsely ground black pepper. Serve immediately on hot dishes, and garnish with the strips of anchovy and a wedge of lemon.

Variation: Use *pissala* (page 173) with fresh garlic and parsley for a similar sauce.

145

TAGLIERINI WITH MUSSELS, RADICCHIO, & ANCHOVY CREAM

3 pounds mussels
A few sprigs fresh parsley
1 bay leaf
A few slices onion or shallot
6 salt-packed anchovies
2 or 3 cloves garlic

4 shallots
2 small heads radicchio
2 tablespoons sweet butter
2 tablespoons virgin olive oil
1 cup heavy cream
Taglierini for 4

Serves 4

WASH AND DE-BEARD the mussels. Steam them open with a little parsley, bay leaf, some onion or shallot, and a little water. Drain the mussels and reserve the juice. Take the mussels out of their shells and set aside. Rinse and filet the anchovies and peel the garlic. Pound the anchovies and garlic in a mortar with a pestle to make a smooth thick paste. Peel and dice the shallots. Cut the radicchio crosswise into thin ribbons. Chop some parsley.

START THE SHALLOTS cooking in a little butter and oil. Add the radicchio and cook until it begins to wilt and change color. Add approximately ½ cup of the mussel juice, the cream, and the anchovy paste. Reduce the sauce slightly but do not allow it to become too thick. Cook the noodles and just before they are ready, add the mussels to the sauce. Add the noodles to the sauce, and toss all together. Season with black pepper and garnish with chopped parsley.

Variation: Put the completed pasta in a shallow gratin dish, cover the top with fresh bread crumbs, and dot with butter. Gratinée the pasta in a very hot oven until the bread crumb top is brown and crisp.

WHITE BEAN & PASTA SOUP

¾ pound dried	2 carrots
cannellini beans	1 stalk celery
A large section of prosciutto	1 onion
bone with some meat and rind	Virgin olive oil
Several sprigs fresh thyme	½ pound fusilli or gemelli
1 bay leaf	Fresh sage leaves
2 quarts chicken stock	Salt and pepper
2 cloves garlic	Rocket leaves (optional)

Serves 4

DRIED PASTA, such as fusilli or gemelli, has a substantial texture and will hold the sauce for this dish well.

Put the beans in a pot of cold water and bring to a boil. Remove them from the fire and drain. Start them cooking again with the prosciutto bone, thyme, bay leaf, and chicken stock. Dice the garlic and the aromatic vegetables and sauté them in ¼ cup or so of olive oil and add to the beans. Simmer gently, covered, for several hours (probably 3), until soft enough to purée. If more liquid is necessary during the cooking, add water as needed. Remove the meat from the prosciutto bone and save to return to the beans. Purée two-thirds of the beans through a sieve or food mill; leaving some beans whole makes a nicely textured sauce.

Combine the purée, the beans, and the prosciutto meat. Add water or stock if needed to thin to the consistency of a thick soup. Return the beans to the stove and keep hot.

Cook the pasta and put it into a pan with some warm olive oil and minced sage. Season with salt and pepper. Add enough of the bean soup to thoroughly coat the noodles, plus some extra. (This dish is more pasta than beans.) Serve in hot soup bowls garnished with ground black pepper and young rocket leaves if you have them.

Variation: Cook tiny French lentils with a mirepoix of vegetables and a bouquet garni in light chicken stock until they are tender but not mushy. Purée half of the beans, then mix the purée and beans. Thin to the consistency of a light soup with more stock or water. Add some cooked, dried pasta, such as torti or mughetto, and simmer briefly. Serve garnished with a little sauce of olive oil, chopped garlic, and parsley. Pass around freshly grated Parmesan at the table.

147

PIZZA & CALZONE

PIZZA DOUGH

Make a sponge by mixing together
 ¼ cup lukewarm water
 2 teaspoons active dry yeast
 ¼ cup rye flour

Let it rise 20 to 30 minutes, then add
 ½ cup lukewarm water
 1 tablespoon milk
 2 tablespoons olive oil
 ½ teaspoon salt
 1¾ cups unbleached all-purpose flour

MIX THE DOUGH with a wooden spoon, then knead on a floured board. It will be soft and a little sticky. Use quick light motions with your hands so the dough won't stick. Add more flour to the board as you knead but no more than is absolutely necessary. A soft moist dough makes a light and very crispy crust. Knead for 10 to 15 minutes to develop strength and elasticity in the dough. Put it in a bowl rubbed with olive oil, and oil the surface of the dough to prevent a crust from forming. Cover the bowl with a towel and put it in a warm place, approximately 90°F to 110°F. An oven heated just by its pilot light is a good spot. Let the dough rise to double its size, for about 2 hours, then punch it down. Let it rise about 40 minutes more, then shape and bake it. This recipe makes one 12-inch to 14-inch pizza, or several small ones.

151

One of the very best ways to bake a pizza is directly on the floor of a wood-fired brick or stone oven. The intense heat of a wood fire can drive the temperature to 500°F or more, and it gives the dough a smoky flavor. When the dough slides onto the hot bricks it reacts instantly: both top and bottom of the pizza cook at once. Not too many households have a brick oven to bake in, but the effect can be approximated by putting a layer of unglazed ceramic tiles on a rack in your oven. Preheat the oven to 450°F to 500°F. Use a wood paddle made especially for the purpose, or the back of a baking sheet, to put the pizza in and remove it from the oven.

Flatten the dough on a heavily floured board. Use a rolling pin to roll the dough to roughly 12 to 14 inches in diameter. The dough should be ⅛- to ¼-inch thick. Transfer the dough to a paddle or baking sheet, also heavily floured. Have your toppings ready, at room temperature, and work quickly putting them on the pizza. After a minute or so it will begin to stick, and will be impossible to slide off the paddle. When garnishing the pizza, anticipate flavor and balance. A light hand with weighty ingredients such as cheese, tomatoes, sausage, and so on, and bold amounts of fresh herbs, garlic, anchovies, flavored oils and the like, works best. It is better to err on the side of flavor. Tomatoes and other wet foods should be drained of excess liquid. Too much weight or moisture on the dough makes it difficult for it to rise and cook well on the bottom. Whatever is on top must be able to cook in 15 minutes, or should have had some partial cooking beforehand. Beware of spilling anything wet or oily between the dough and paddle, as that too will prevent it from sliding. Give the paddle a few shakes back and forth to make sure the dough is loose. Slide the pizza from the paddle onto the hot tiles in the oven with abrupt jerking motions of your wrist. This takes a certain knack but comes easily after a few tries. The pizza will be browned and cooked in 12 to 15 minutes.

When you roll and shape the dough, feel free to make it any shape you wish. Large flat pizzas with uneven bubbly edges have a rustic appeal. Small individual-sized pizzas, served as a savory accompaniment to a meal, instead of bread, are very satisfying.

If your oven cannot maintain an intense heat of 450°F to 500°F, then the dough will perform better if rolled a little on the thick side, ¼-inch or more. When the dough is rolled thin and requires 20 to 25 minutes to cook at some temperature less than 450°F, then it tends to have a cracker-like texture. A thicker dough allows for a bready interior and a crusty exterior. When you are deciding if the pizza is cooked, check the bottom to make sure it is quite crisp. The crust always softens a bit when it cools down. The real purpose of the tiles is to make a good texture on the bottom of the pizza.

Caramelized Onions, Gorgonzola, & Rosemary

Gently cook 4 thinly sliced onions in some butter and olive oil, with salt and pepper, for about an hour, until brown and caramelized. Spread the dough with the onions, dot with ¼ pound Gorgonzola and sprinkle lightly with finely chopped rosemary. Bake and serve garnished with freshly ground black pepper.

Onions, Garlic, & Herbs

Sauté 3 or 4 sliced onions and lots of sliced garlic in olive oil until just softened. Use this as the base of the pizza topping. Finely chop a mixture of herbs such as parsley, thyme, oregano, basil, and rosemary. Sprinkle these over the onions, and season with salt and pepper. Put the pizza in the oven. Halfway through the baking, cover the top with a light layer of freshly grated Parmesan and Romano cheeses, mixed. When it comes out of the oven, drizzle olive oil over the crusty edges.

Onion Confit, Walnuts, & Anchovies

Shape the pizza dough and cover the top with a layer of onion confit (see page 123). Put the pizza in the oven, and halfway through the baking sprinkle a handful of roughly chopped walnuts over the onions. When it is cooked, remove the pizza from the oven and garnish with strips of anchovy filet and slices of hard-cooked egg.

Pissaladière

The classic onion and anchovy pizza, or tart, has its origin in the anchovy paste, or pissala (see page 173). Sauté 4 or 5 onions in olive oil with thyme and salt and pepper. Spread the pizza dough with a light layer of pissala, and cover with a thick layer of onions, strips of anchovy filet, and black pepper. Bake the pizza.

153

Stewed Whole Garlic

Peel the cloves of several heads of garlic and stew them slowly in olive oil, stirring constantly, until soft and beginning to caramelize, about 15 to 20 minutes. Soften a sliced red onion in olive oil. Spread these over the dough and bake it. When it comes from the oven, drizzle with olive oil and garnish with strips of anchovy filets, chopped marjoram, and black pepper.

Stewed Garlic, Pancetta, & Herbs

Use lots of stewed garlic, as above, thin slices of pancetta cut in pieces, olive oil, and mixed chopped herbs.

Stewed Garlic, Pancetta, & Artichoke Hearts

Use whole stewed garlic, the same as above, with very thin slices of pancetta cut in pieces, and artichoke hearts sliced and blanched, then tossed in olive oil. Halfway through the baking, add some freshly grated Parmesan cheese.

Roasted Garlic Purée & Chanterelles

Separate the cloves of several heads of garlic. Toss the cloves, in their skins, in olive oil. Put them in a roasting pan, season with salt and pepper, bay leaves, and fresh thyme branches. Cover the pan with foil and bake in a 300°F oven for approximately 1½ hours, until the garlic is very soft. Put the garlic through a food mill. Spread this purée over the pizza dough and cover it with sliced chanterelles that have been lightly sautéed in butter. Bake the pizza and garnish it with chopped fresh parsley.

Leeks, Pancetta, & Goat Cheese

Stew 2 dozen baby leeks or the white parts of 5 or 6 full-sized leeks in butter until tender. Season with salt and pepper and some thyme leaves. When the leeks are cool, crumble 3 ounces or so of fresh Sonoma goat cheese and mix with the leeks. Spread this mixture over the top of the pizza dough and top that with 3 thin slices of pancetta, cut into small pieces. Bake the pizza, and when cooked, garnish with a little virgin olive oil.

Grilled Eggplant & Pesto

Thinly slice 5 or 6 small Japanese eggplants. Brush them with olive oil and charcoal grill them until lightly browned on both sides. Roll the dough and moisten it with a light coating of pesto sauce (see page 70). Arrange the eggplant slices on the dough and bake the pizza. Brush the eggplant with pesto when the pizza is done.

Eggplant, Tomatoes, & Parmesan

Cut 4 or 5 small eggplants into a julienne. Sauté the eggplant in hot olive oil 5 or 6 minutes, until it softens and browns. At the last minute add 5 or 6 cloves of sliced garlic and season with salt and pepper. Quarter about 1½ cups of Sweet 100 cherry tomatoes. Roll the pizza dough and brush it with olive oil. Spread the tomatoes over it. Salt them, then cover with the eggplant and garlic. Cover the eggplant with shaved Parmesan cheese and bake the pizza. Garnish with purple basil leaves.

Roasted Eggplant & Mozzarella

Slice one large or several small Japanese eggplants in ⅛- to ¼-inch slices. Brush them with olive oil, season with salt and pepper, put them in a single layer on a roasting pan, and bake in a hot oven until nicely browned. Or grill the slices over a charcoal fire. Roll the dough and sprinkle it with a little finely chopped garlic, and a light layer of grated mozzarella cheese, about ¼ pound. Arrange the eggplant slices on the cheese, sprinkle just a little more cheese over the eggplant, and bake the pizza. Garnish it from the oven with some chopped fresh marjoram.

Eggplant & Dried Tomato Purée

Make a purée of about a dozen or so dried tomato halves and as much olive oil as needed to make them smooth. Roll the pizza dough and spread the purée over the surface. Cover the dough with a sliced sautéed onion, a little chopped garlic, and a single layer of roasted eggplant slices. Bake the pizza and garnish with olive oil, chopped parsley, and black pepper.

Dried Tomato Purée & Mozzarella

Make a purée of dried tomatoes and olive oil. Roll the pizza dough and spread it with the purée. Add a light layer of sautéed onions. Top with thin slices of mozzarella cheese. Garnish the top with Niçoise olives, and bake.

Multicolored Peppers & Fresh Sausage

Sauté a mixture of 4 or 5 peppers: sweet red bells, yellow, green, brown, Anaheim, or whatever you have. Cook them with a sliced red onion and some garlic. Season with salt and pepper and some fresh herbs. Put this mixture on the pizza dough and dot with bits of fresh sausage, about ¼ pound (any sort of good freshly ground pork sausage, flavored with garlic, fennel, wine, etc., will do). When the pizza is hot from the oven, garnish with freshly grated Parmesan cheese.

Hot Peppers, Coriander, & Sausage

Sauté a mixture of peppers such as poblano chiles, Anaheim peppers, bell peppers, and jalapeños with some red onion and garlic. Spread the softened peppers over the pizza dough and arrange thin slices of sausage over the top. Try different kinds of sausage (sweet fresh pork sausage, spicy chorizo, hot Calabrese, etc.). When the pizza is cooked, garnish with some grated dry jack cheese and leaves of fresh coriander.

Roasted Tomato Sauce

Core 10 tomatoes, rub them with olive oil, season with salt, and roast them in a hot oven (or charcoal grill them) until the skins are browned and blistered. Sauté a finely chopped onion and several sliced cloves of garlic in olive oil for a few minutes. Add the tomatoes and cook them down to a thick paste. Roll the pizza to whatever shape you want, spread it with the tomato sauce, and bake it. Garnish this pizza with any number of things – strips of anchovy, herbs, black olives, fried squid, shaved Parmesan . . .

Tomatoes, Herbs, & Quail Eggs

Slice some ripe tomatoes and drain them of their excess juice. Finely chop a mixture of herbs such as green and purple basil, marjoram, parsley, and chervil. Mince a few garlic cloves. Boil 10 or 12 quail eggs. Start them in a pan of cold water, bring to a boil, boil ½ minute, and run them under cold water. Brush the dough with olive oil. Arrange the tomato slices on the dough, season with salt and pepper, herbs, and garlic, and bake. Remove it from the oven, and garnish with slices of quail eggs, strips of anchovy if you like, a little more of the herb mixture, and olive oil.

Fresh Mozzarella, Tomatoes, & Basil

Put a layer of lightly sautéed sliced red onion on the dough. Cover with a layer of ripe tomatoes, thinly sliced and drained of their juice and seeds. Season with salt and pepper and a sprinkling of finely chopped garlic. Then put matchstick-sized pieces of fresh mozzarella in and around the tomatoes. When the pizza is done, drizzle with virgin olive oil, and garnish with a chiffonade of basil.

Dried Tomatoes, Mozzarella, & Olives

Roll the dough, brush it with olive oil, and cover with a light layer of grated mozzarella. Sprinkle the cheese with a small handful of slivered dried tomatoes and some finely chopped garlic. Cook the pizza for 6 to 8 minutes, then sprinkle a little more cheese over the top to protect the tomatoes and garlic. Finish baking, and garnish with pitted and chopped black olives.

Fresh & Dried Wild Mushrooms

Soak a handful of dried porcini mushrooms (*Boletus edulis*) in enough hot water to cover, until soft. Carefully sort through them and remove any pockets of dirt or grit. Chop them. Thinly slice ¾ pound of fresh cultivated mushrooms. Sauté the mushrooms together in olive oil. Season with salt and pepper, and add some minced garlic and chopped parsley. Roll the dough and top with the mushroom mixture. Add 5 or 6 dried tomatoes, slivered, and a light layer of freshly grated Parmesan. Put the pizza in the oven. Halfway through the baking, add some more Parmesan. When the pizza is removed from the oven, brush the crusty edges with olive oil.

Pancetta, Mushrooms, & Garlic

Sauté ¾ pound of sliced fresh mushrooms (or a combination of dried and fresh wild mushrooms) with some garlic, fresh thyme, and parsley. Cut 5 ounces or so of pancetta into little lardoons and cook them until soft, to render the fat. Roll the dough and top with the mushrooms and pancetta. Bake the pizza, and when it is done, garnish with some grated dry jack cheese.

Wild Mushrooms

Sauté ½ pound of chanterelles, or any combination of wild mushrooms, in a mixture of butter and olive oil, with garlic and parsley. Or grill whole chanterelles or cèpes, then slice them and toss with a little oil, chopped garlic, and chopped herbs. Top the dough with the mushrooms and bake it.

Crawfish Tails & Yellow Tomatoes

Boil 2 dozen live crawfish in seasoned water. Separate the tails and claws and shell them. Make a sauce from the shells and bodies with aromatic vegetables and herbs and water (see page 98). Strain it, season with Cognac and lemon, and reduce to a concentrated essence. Soften a sliced onion in butter with thyme. Start with these onions on the dough, then put on a light layer of peeled and seeded yellow tomatoes and moisten with 2 tablespoons of the crawfish reduction. Put the pizza in the oven. A minute or two before it is done, strew the tails and claws, which have been marinating in the reduction, all over the top and finish baking. Garnish with chopped parsley before sending it to the table.

Fennel & Mussels

Steam open some mussels and remove them from the shells. Lightly coat with a mixture of fresh bread crumbs, olive oil, and Pernod. Peel, seed, and chop a few tomatoes. Mix them with finely chopped garlic and salt and pepper. Put a layer of tomatoes on the dough; add the mussels and small sprigs of fennel tops. Drizzle with a little olive oil and bake.

Squid & Red Peppers

Slice 2 or 3 sweet red peppers and sauté them in a little olive oil. Clean and thinly slice a pound of fresh squid and season with salt and pepper. Fry the squid in very hot olive oil for 30 to 40 seconds. Chop some garlic and mix it with the peppers. Roll the dough and top it with the peppers, squid, and some pitted black olives. Bake the pizza, and garnish with chopped basil, parsley, and a little virgin olive oil.

159

Shrimp, Green Onion, & Tomato

Cut 6 green onions into 1-inch sections and cook gently for 1 minute in olive oil. Add ¾ pound shelled fresh shrimp and some chopped garlic, and remove from the heat. Toss all together and season with salt and pepper. Peel, seed, and chop 2 tomatoes. Roll the dough and brush it with olive oil. Make a layer of tomatoes, then add the shrimp and onions. Bake the pizza until crusty and golden, and garnish the shrimp with chopped basil and parsley. Try this pizza with a mixture of shellfish: squid tentacles, shrimp, mussels, scallops, and so on.

Truffle Pizza

Roll the dough very thin so that it will cook very fast. Brush with olive oil and shave thin slices of white truffle all over the surface. Cover the truffles with grated or thinly sliced fine Italian fontina cheese, just enough to protect the truffles in the oven. Shavings of young moist Parmesan instead of fontina are also very good. The cheese should be just melted when the crust is done.

Fresh Anchovies, Garlic, & Red Onions

Clean and filet some fresh anchovies (about 18), and marinate them in a little olive oil. Sauté 2 thinly sliced red onions in olive oil. Season with salt and pepper and some chopped mixed herbs (parsley, basil, marjoram, fennel, etc.). Make a layer of the onions on the pizza dough. Sprinkle on some chopped garlic and cover with the fresh anchovies. Season with salt and pepper and bake. Eat the pizza as is, or garnish with strips of roasted peppers, olives, red pepper oil, chopped tomato, and so on.

Roasted New Potatoes & Pesto

Slice 7 or 8 new potatoes, toss them in olive oil, season with salt and pepper, and roast in a hot oven until brown. Spread the pesto sauce (see page 70), which should be a little on the oily side, over the pizza dough. Cover that with the roasted potato slices and perhaps whole young garlic cloves fried in their skins. Bake the pizza, and when it is done dribble more pesto sauce over the top.

Fresh Herbs

Make small individual pizzas to use for hors d'oeuvres, or instead of bread, to accompany a meal. Brush the dough with a fine virgin olive oil, sprinkle generously with freshly chopped mixed herbs, and season with salt and pepper. Drizzle with more oil when it is hot from the oven. Baked this way, with very little on it, the dough becomes very crisp and delicate.

Tapenade & Mozzarella

Tapenade is a paste made of pitted ripe black olives, such as the Gaeta or Niçoise type, anchovies, and garlic, seasoned with a little Cognac (see page 42). Spread the pizza with the sauce. Cover with a light layer of grated mozzarella and bake. Garnish with Niçoise olives tossed in olive oil and fresh orange zest.

Escarole, Capers, & Fontina

Stew 2 bunches of roughly chopped escarole greens with an onion and 6 or 7 cloves of garlic in olive oil until soft. Season with salt and pepper and enough red wine vinegar to make them sharp to the taste. Put a layer of greens on the pizza dough. Sprinkle with pitted black olives, capers rinsed of their brine, and a mixture of grated mozzarella and fontina cheeses. Take care to bake long enough to make the bottom crispy.

Grilled Radicchio & Pancetta

Cut 2 heads of radicchio in quarters, brush them with olive oil, season, and charcoal grill them. Cut them in thin strips. Grill 5 to 6 pancetta slices, then cut in small pieces. Roast 2 sweet red peppers over the charcoal fire. Peel and seed them and cut into thin strips. Chop a little anchovy and garlic and mix with olive oil and a little red wine vinegar. Toss the radicchio, pancetta, and peppers in the dressing, top the pizza dough with this mixture, season with black pepper, and bake the pizza.

Duck Confit & Pearl Onions

Use any leftover bits and pieces of duck confit (see page 176), skin and gizzards as well, that you might have. Cook a quantity of tiny pearl onions in butter and good stock, duck or pigeon, until they are tender and caramelized and coated with the glaze of reduced stock. Stir in the confit and cover the pizza dough with this mixture. Bake the pizza, and sprinkle with chopped parsley when it is done. Open a bottle of good red wine.

Grilled Artichokes, Pancetta, & Thyme

Soften a sliced onion in olive oil with 2 tablespoons of fresh thyme leaves. Trim 1 pound of tiny artichokes down to the heart, cut them in half, marinate in olive oil for an hour, and then charcoal grill them until tender and browned. Cut the halves into quarters and season with salt and pepper. Cut 5 or 6 pancetta slices in lardoons and cook them a little to render the fat. Roll the dough and spread it with the onions and thyme. Top that with the artichokes and pancetta, and bake.

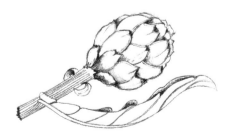

CHEZ PANISSE CALZONE

2 ounces fresh Sonoma goat cheese
2 ounces French goat cheese, such as Bûcheron or Lezay
7 ounces mozzarella
2 slices prosciutto
2 tablespoons fresh chives
2 tablespoons fresh parsley
1 sprig each fresh thyme and marjoram
2 small cloves garlic
Black pepper
Pizza dough

CALZONE IS on the Café menu every day at Chez Panisse. The term actually refers to the form of the pizza: a turnover with the filling enclosed. This version is a combination of mild and tangy cheeses, prosciutto, garlic, and herbs.

Crumble the goat cheeses and grate the mozzarella. Cut 2 slices of prosciutto, about twice as thick as you would serve for a sandwich or salad, into a julienne. Finely cut 2 tablespoons of chives and mince the same amount of parsley. Chop the leaves of a small sprig each of thyme and marjoram. Mince the garlic. Blend all of these ingredients together and season with some coarsely ground black pepper.

Roll the pizza dough in one large circle, 14 inches in diameter, or divide the dough in 2 or 3 pieces and make small calzoni. Put the filling on one-half of the dough, leaving an inch of margin space at the edge. Moisten the edge with water and fold the other half of the dough over the filling to make the edges meet. Fold the dough at the edges up onto itself to form a sort of running curl, pinching as you go along to seal it tight. Put it onto the floured paddle and slide it in the oven. Bake for approximately 15 to 18 minutes, until it is quite brown and crisp. Remove it from the oven and brush the top with olive oil. Serve it whole and cut with a serrated knife at the table.

GARDEN NOTES
GLOSSARY
INDEX

Garden Notes

Chives are perennials. They should be cut back two or three times a year to force tender new growth. Chives become scraggly after the second year, and are better if replaced by new plants every other season.

Fava beans, also called broad beans and horse beans, are usually grown only in the spring because hot weather spoils their flavor. In very mild climates you can grow them later in the season. They grow tall, 4 feet or more, and do best if given some kind of support. The flowers are beautiful white blossoms, like sweet peas with black centers. They appear 6 weeks or so after planting, and beans develop soon thereafter. The Italians eat the young beans raw, seasoned with salt and pepper and dipped in olive oil, and they are absolutely delicious this way. Fava beans are sometimes planted as a cover crop because they add nitrogen to the soil. Plant the seeds 2 inches deep and 4 to 5 inches apart.

Garlic is slow-growing but very hardy. Save cloves of whatever garlic you find particularly tasty. The small heads with deep rose-colored skins taste wonderful. When the cloves begin to sprout, plant them about 1½ inches deep in loose, but not overly rich, soil about 4 inches apart. Plant continually from spring to fall to have many plants at different stages of maturity. They are ready to be harvested from 5 to 9 months after planting. In California the commercial growers usually plant in October or November and harvest in June or July. The young green garlic called for in the recipes had been in the ground about 6 months. It is not dried, but cooked while still fresh and green.

Green beans should be picked when they are very small, about 2 to 3 inches long. Bush beans do not require the support of a trellis. Démonchaux (see page 169) sells a few varieties of true *haricots verts*: Fin de Bagnols, Triomphe de Farcy, and Radar. Blue Lake beans are delectable when harvested young. Royalty Purple Pod is another interesting variety; the plants are quite beautiful with purple stems and flowers. The beans themselves are deep purple, giving them the great advantage of being easily picked. Surprisingly, they do not remain purple when cooked, but turn a brilliant green. These bush beans grow about 2 feet tall and come into full production 6 to 8 weeks after planting. They can be grown from spring to fall as long as the weather is warm.

Green Onions, or bunching onions, are grown from seed. (There is a good French variety that is red.) Plant seeds close together in rows, and thin as they mature: the little trimmings are quite delicious. Like the rest of the onion family, they like full sun, heat, regular waterings, and loose sandy soil with good drainage.

Herbs, massed in a bed or border, are extremely beautiful. Given a little water, most herbs are quite self-sufficient. They do not require special or rich soil, and they love heat. The plants commonly sold in supermarkets and nurseries in 2-inch containers, planted in spring or early summer, by the following year will have increased in size about 10 times. Some perennial herbs particularly useful in the kitchen are: silver thyme, English thyme, French or leaf thyme, lemon thyme, marjoram, red marjoram, sage, variegated sage, oregano, tarragon, winter savory, sorrel, rosemary, lovage, hyssop, fennel, and borage. Annual herbs require more attention and are better grown in culti-vated beds in large quantities: curly-leafed and Italian flat leaf parsley, chervil, basil, purple or opal basil, dwarf basil, and summer savory. Large plots of parsley grown from seed, like lettuce, work very well. Chervil is very delicate and is happy under a tree or in partial shade. Basil is easy to grow from seed and loves the heat, but is quite vulnerable to the cold; it is one of the first casualties when the weather changes in the fall. Purple basil tastes almost like anise, and is exciting to grow because it is so gorgeous. Dwarf basil has a more peppery flavor than the large-leaf varieties and its aroma is suggestive of roses.

Lettuces of most varieties should be grown like rocket in a rich light soil of fine texture. It is worthwhile to prepare the beds very carefully with a mixture of fertilizer, fine compost, humus, sand, and soil. Work the bed until the surface is very smooth and loose. Lettuce seeds are minuscule and require a delicate environment to germinate success-fully. One method is to sow the seeds evenly over the surface of the prepared bed and then barely cover them with commercial potting soil or carefully sifted compost. Keep the bed moist until the seeds have sprouted, usually in 10 to 14 days. Lettuce can be harvested by picking the outer leaves when they are 3 to 4 inches tall, leaving the roots and inner leaves to continue producing. The Provençal term *mesclun* refers to a mixture of lettuces planted together. It usually includes rocket, chervil, red and green lettuces, chicory, dandelion, and a peppery garden cress. The best source we know of in this country for lettuce seeds, as well as many imported French vegetable and herb varieties, is Herb Gathering, Inc. (formerly J. A. Démonchaux Co.), 5742 Kenwood, Kansas City, Missouri 64110. They list rocket, chervil, garden cress, endives, Marvel of Four Seasons (a beautiful red lettuce), Romaine Ballon, red romaine, oak leaf, Augusta, *mâche* (corn salad or lamb's-lettuce), and others. Their catalogue is enough to inspire a very ambitious garden.

Nasturtiums are independent flowers: they require no special soil or care, and they have a trailing habit and will climb, if given an opportunity. Too much heat is difficult for them. They do well in a moist, partially shaded spot, under a tree or at the edge of a border.

Peas, like fava beans, are very sensitive to heat and only grow well in the cool springtime. Plant them 2 inches deep in rich, fast-draining soil as early as the ground can be worked. In mild winter climates, plant from September through February. Climbing peas require the support of a trellis, but they are more prolific and have a longer season than the bush or dwarf peas. Sugar snap peas are a cross between snow peas and peas, and have a greater heat tolerance. Kelvedon is an exceptional variety. When harvesting peas, be sure to pick all of the pods as they are ready; if allowed to mature completely the plant will stop producing.

Peppers require plenty of hot sun to mature properly. Red bell peppers are simply green bell peppers left on the vine to ripen completely. Anaheim peppers, both red and green, have a combination of spicy and sweet flavors. Yellow, brown, and purple bells are also available, and they are extraordinary.

Potatoes are at their best small and fresh. There are not too many things better than little new potatoes right out of the garden. Seed potatoes are readily available in local nurseries and from seed catalogues. Besides red, white, and russet potatoes, two interesting varieties are Yellow Swedish and Rose Fir. Potatoes like a lot of space and loose deep soil. An addition of fertilizer rich in potash is especially stimulating. Growing time is reduced by several weeks if the seed potatoes are allowed to sprout before being planted. Cut the potatoes

169

in pieces, each with 1 or 2 strong sprouts, and plant them about 4 inches deep, 8 to 10 inches apart. They are ready to harvest when the plants begin to flower.

Radishes are easy and satisfying to grow. Almost every seed germinates, and they pop up 4 to 7 days after planting. They should be planted in loose soft soil and when they have sprouted and the leaves begin to grow, mound the dirt up around the little stalks so that the developing radish will be well covered. They are ready to eat in about 2 weeks.

Rocket, roquette, and arugula are all names for the same plant. It has a hot peppery, nutty flavor, suggestive of walnuts. Scatter the seeds, sowing densely, on a rich well-worked bed, and just barely cover with a layer of fine soil. Keep the bed moist, watering a couple of times a day, and the seeds will germinate in less than a week. Successive small plantings about one month apart work very well. Rocket grows fast and in two weeks it is ready to eat. Pick the outer leaves; the inner ones will flourish. The older the plant, the more peppery its flavor. Rocket cannot tolerate real heat; in summer it will go to seed very rapidly.

Shallots are tricky to grow. They require very sandy soil with excellent drainage and are best grown from sets – tiny bulbs. Once they have sprouted, brush away the dirt from all but the lower root end of the bulb, so they will not rot from too much moisture. They can be planted almost any time of year in fine weather. Planted in early spring, they can be harvested about 12 weeks later.

Squash varieties are numerous. Our familiar zucchini is rather banal compared to the tastier varieties grown by the French and Italians. Their courgettes are pale green with dark stripes and bulbous ends. Herb Gathering, Inc. sells seeds for two varieties of this sort, Ambassador and Aristocrat. One plant each of zucchini, yellow crookneck, and summer squash is a lot to keep up with, but nice for variety. Pick the squash while they are small with the flowers still fresh and open. The plants will produce many more flowers than squash. This means many flowers for stuffing and frying, squash and squash blossom soup, and pasta.

Swiss chard and red chard are hardy and productive. Pick the outer leaves consistently to keep the new leaves coming and to prevent the plant from bolting. Chard and spinach planted in late summer will winter over in mild climates and provide greens into late fall.

Tomatoes come in so many varieties that you should experiment to find the right ones for your climate and growing season. Here are some varieties with exceptional flavor we have grown in California: Jubilee, a large, luminous golden tomato; Sweet 100, a tiny red cherry tomato with intensely sweet fruit; Yellow Pear, a cherry tomato with a self-explanatory name; Early Girl, a medium-sized, early-ripening variety; Marmande, available from Herb Gathering, Inc., an Old World non-hybridized tomato, large and squat, with deep uneven ridges; Roma and San Marzano, pear-shaped, thick-skinned, fleshy tomatoes with few seeds (these are excellent for drying). Beware of overwatering tomatoes, especially during the very early development of the fruit.

Glossary of Ingredients

Anchovies in this book means whole anchovies packed in salt. Commercially available anchovies are also fileted and packed in oil, smoked and canned, dried, or reduced to a paste and sold in tubes, but you should avoid these products. Whole fish under salt look like small silvery fish, and since they are still on the bone, are much more flavorful and, paradoxically, much less salty than oil-packed filets. European salt-packed anchovies come from Sicily, Portugal, and Spain; but various species of anchovies are found all over the world (16 species in American waters alone).

Since fresh anchovies are sometimes available in the spring and summer, you may wish to salt cure your own. The fresh fish are first beheaded, gutted, and rinsed. Then they are layered with pure coarse salt (iodized salt makes them mushy) and left for up to 24 hours. After they have exuded some of their juices, they are drained and blotted dry; then repacked, crosshatched between ½-inch layers of salt (sometimes with some crushed peppercorns); weighted; and left in a cool place for 5 or 6 days. They will release enough liquid to form a brine which prevents the growth of microorganisms, and some of their oil will rise to the surface. This must be skimmed off or it will turn rancid. Then the sterilized jars are sealed and refrigerated, where they will keep for up to 2 years.

When you open a can of salt-packed anchovies, it is always a good idea to repack those you don't use under a fresh layer of coarse salt, and then cover the can airtight with plastic wrap. Exposed to air, anchovies rapidly start to taste strange. Even fileted and kept in olive oil in the refrigerator they lose quality.

Here is Martine's Provençal recipe for *pissala* (or *pissalat*), a homemade anchovy paste: Behead, gut, and rinse some anchovies. Layer them in a large jar between layers of pure coarse salt, fresh thyme, bay, fennel, and crushed peppercorns (of different colors). The salt layers should be light. Every day for a month mix the *pissala* by stirring with a wooden spoon; this prevents the oil from standing on the surface and going rancid. After a month, lift the fish from the brine and mash through a sieve or strain through a food mill to make a very smooth purée. Pack in a jar, cover the top with an inch or so of olive oil, and store in the refrigerator.

Asparagus is found in the markets for many months. It is best in late winter and early spring. Asparagus roots are dormant in winter and send up shoots in the spring, and the first few harvests are the most succulent. The buds should be of good color, moist, and compact. Large fat asparagus, as fresh as possible, are the most delicious. Some varieties of asparagus are sometimes earthed up and blanched, especially in Europe. The asparagus that results is purple at the tips, white on its stalk, and particularly fine flavored. Fat asparagus, white or green, should be peeled.

Caviar means fish eggs, especially the roe of different species of sturgeon. Russian caviar is named after the Caspian Sea sturgeon from which it is taken: Beluga, generally considered the finest, has the largest eggs and the most delicate flavor; Osetra has stronger-flavored, yellow-brown eggs (rather than gray); and Sevruga has the strongest-flavored eggs of all. There are several species of sturgeon in American waters, of which the white sturgeon of the Pacific Coast reputedly has the finest caviar. The commercial fishery of sturgeon is illegal in California, but American caviar from Washington and Oregon is marketed.

Whatever its origin, the best caviar is very fresh and lightly salted, and the eggs are distinct, crisp, and firm. When caviar is processed, the roe sac is slit open and the eggs are inspected and cleaned. They are then pushed through a screen or cotton sieve to separate them and leave any membrane behind. They are left in a brine for 15 to 20 minutes; and finally drained well, salted, and packed in tins or jars. (Some caviar is pasteurized at this point; after cooking it is no longer fresh, and the flavor suffers.) Fresh Russian caviar marked *malossol* ("little salt") will have had the least salt added and will be delicate, but perishable. Kept at 28°F and sealed airtight, caviar will keep a month. Once exposed to air, the eggs start to break down and lose their briny, oysterlike smell. (However, if you make your own caviar you shouldn't eat it for at least 2 days; experts say the eggs "fret" and need time to be more "at ease.")

Golden caviar is the name given to whitefish roe from the Great Lakes. It is highly perishable, and the eggs collapse almost immediately if not frozen. Buy it frozen or just thawed, and eat it as soon as possible.

Salmon roe, sometimes called red caviar, can come from any of the various Pacific Coast salmon. The lightest and most delicate is from chum salmon. Silver salmon roe is dark red and stronger, and king salmon roe is rather oily and stronger yet. To make your own salmon caviar, slit open the roe sac and gently press the eggs through a ¼-inch mesh netting stretched taut over a bowl. Add the eggs to a brine, gently swirl them around to loosen any membrane, and leave, refrigerated, for 15 to 20 minutes. (The length of the soak and the strength of the brine depend on the eggs: the older they are, the oilier, and the more salt they will absorb. Start with a solution of 1 part salt to 5 parts water, and keep tasting.) Lift off any bits of membrane that may have floated to the surface; drain the eggs in a sieve over a bowl, and refrigerate for about an hour; then pack the eggs carefully into small sterilized jars. Cover tightly and refrigerate. Let the eggs rest for 2 days. They will keep for a month or more unopened; once opened, eat them within a week.

Charcoal, as referred to in this book, is real mesquite charcoal from Mexico. This product is available in many grocery and hardware stores. It burns slowly and very hot, and adds a pleasant smoky flavor to the food. Do not use lighter fluid, or whatever you grill will have a very unpleasant taste and smell.

Chiffonade applies to leafy ingredients that are cut into narrow or wide ribbons for an evenly shredded effect. One way of doing this is to make little stacks of, say, basil leaves, and cut across and down through the stack at even intervals. For such things as radicchio, cut the head in half lengthwise, place the cut side down on the cutting board and slice straight through the layers of leaves at even intervals.

Cranberry beans, when fresh, have green pods streaked with red. The young beans are still pale green, very moist and crispy, and not starchy tasting. They are excellent raw in salad with olive oil, salt, pepper, and savory. The more mature bean is white, plump, and roundish, with red streaks. At both stages of maturity they are great with pasta.

Crème fraîche is easily made if you mix 2 cups fresh sweet cream and 1 tablespoon buttermilk, then cover the bowl with a cloth and let it sit 24 to 36 hours at room temperature. By then it will have thickened. Stir the cream until it is very smooth. Cover and refrigerate. It will keep very well for a week or two. Its tangy flavor will become stronger and its consistency thicker the older it is. If so desired, more fresh cream can be added to dilute the mixture and to continue the culture.

Duck confit is made like this: Remove the backbone from a 4 to 5 pound duck and cut the duck into 4 pieces. Mix together a cup of coarse salt, a few crushed bay leaves, and 2 teaspoons dried thyme. Rub the duck with the salt and herb mixture and put it in an earthenware crock. Sprinkle the remaining salt on top, cover the duck, and weight it. Leave it in a cool place or refrigerate for 1 to 2 days.

To finish the confit, remove the duck from the cure and wipe each piece clean with a towel. Melt about 6 cups duck or goose fat in a pan that will hold the duck pieces snugly in one layer. (The fat should cover the duck.) When the fat is hot, add the duck pieces and a bouquet garni of some parsley stems, black peppercorns, and a head of garlic cut in half crosswise. Simmer gently for about 1½ hours. Test for doneness by inserting a skewer through the thickest part of the leg; it should pass through with no resistance.

Remove the duck from the fat and let it cool. Carefully pour the fat through a fine strainer, taking care to stop before getting to the juices and debris which have settled to the bottom. Clarify the fat by boiling to remove any liquids, skimming frequently. Watch carefully that it does not brown. When it is clean, strain it again and let it cool to room temperature. When the duck is cool, pack the pieces in an earthenware crock. Pour the cooled fat over the duck and refrigerate.

The confit can be kept refrigerated for up to 6 months. It is usable at any time, but the flavor improves if it is aged a few months. If it is to be kept for some time, it is very important that the fat be well clarified and that the duck be well packed in the crock, completely covered with fat.

To cook the preserved duck, remove the pieces from the fat and let them warm to room temperature. Heat a cast-iron skillet over medium heat and cook the duck pieces skin side down for 10 to 15 minutes, until they are browned and heated through.

Dungeness crab is the principal crab on the West Coast. On the Atlantic and Gulf coasts the blue crab or other varieties are more likely to be available still alive. Whenever possible, buy live crabs. Pick them up. Choose ones that are lively, feisty, and heavy in relation to their size. If you buy a cooked crab, it is impossible to know how long ago it was cooked and whether or not it was still alive when boiled. The sweet flavor of a crab taken from the sea only a few hours before being boiled alive bears little resemblance to that of one several days out of the water, which may have expired long before cooking.

To cook Dungeness crabs, boil them rapidly for 6 or 7 minutes in a large pot of water seasoned with salt, parsley, lemon, and bay leaf. (The water should be about as salty as sea water.) Drain the crabs and let them cool. To clean them, separate the body from the top shell, rinse well, and remove and discard the gills and the mouth parts. Twist off the legs from the body, then split it in half where there is a natural break down the center. Crack the shells and remove the meat. One crab will yield approximately 1½ cups of crab meat.

Fava beans are a beautiful brilliant green and, like peas, have a very short season in the spring when they are sweet and juicy and not starchy. Picked young enough, they can be shelled and eaten raw, skin and all. When they are a little older and the skin is no longer bright green, they must be skinned. A good way to do this is to blanch the shelled beans for a minute or so in boiling water. Drain them and allow to cool. Use your thumbnail to pull open the sprout end and squeeze the bean out of its skin. It will pop right out. Once you get the hang of it, this goes very quickly.

Fontina is an Italian semisoft cheese from the Val d'Aosta near Mount Fontin. When properly aged and nicely ripe it is delicious, with a rich nutty flavor. Too often it is sold too firm and underripe. Fontina has a nice texture when melted and cooked.

Garlic will taste different according to when it is harvested and how long it has been stored. Most of the garlic sold in this country is harvested in California in July. Fresh Mexican red garlic appears in the markets in March. Immature garlic can be harvested green in April and May. Garlic used raw should be as fresh as possible. As it dries and ages, its flavor becomes stronger, and by winter it is better used cooked. If the cloves have begun to sprout, the green germ in the center will be bitter; better to split open the cloves and remove the green part before cooking with old garlic.

When buying garlic, choose firm heads without brown or shriveled cloves. Store in a dry, dark, and airy place. Young fresh green garlic can be stored in the refrigerator for one to two months without drying out.

When cooking, peel and chop garlic at the last minute: it oxidizes very fast and its flavor will be spoiled.

Gorgonzola is a blue-veined cheese made from cow's milk from the town of the same name in Lombardy. Dolcelatte ("sweet milk") is the rich creamy kind used in the recipes in this book. Beware of the cheese that has turned or has off-flavors from improper shipping, storage, or overaging. Always taste before buying.

Julienne applies to vegetables cut into matchstick-sized pieces. To do this with a carrot, for example, peel the carrot and divide into sections approximately 2½ to 3 inches long. With a chef's knife, cut a thin slice down the side and length of the carrot. Turn the cut side down on the board so the carrot is resting flat. Square off the other sides. Make parallel lengthwise slices of the desired thickness. Stack those squared slices and cut them into matchsticklike pieces. Save the uneven slices for other uses.

Mascarpone is a very rich fresh Italian cream cheese. It should be almost sweet with a little tang and a texture that resembles thickly beaten whipped cream. It is often served as a dessert – by itself, with some fruit, or layered with Gorgonzola.

Mirepoix means a mixture of vegetables cut into small cubes. The method here is the same as for a julienne with the addition of a final step. Cut the matchstick lengths of vegetables crosswise into even cubes. The usual combination is carrots, onion, and celery.

Mozzarella was originally made from buffalo's milk in the Campagna region of Italy. American versions are made with cow's milk. Some small producers are making very good fresh mozzarella that is still moist and sometimes packed in its own whey. It is much closer to the real thing than the bland overprocessed loaves generally available.

Olives are cultivated principally in Mediterranean countries and in California. Our olives are generally inferior because the Central Valley climate is too hot year round, and the olives develop fatty acids and lose their fruitiness. All olives ripen from green to red to purple to black and can be picked and cured either when green or when red-ripe or black-ripe. There are basically two cures for olives: wet (lye and brine or brine alone) and dry (salt). Wet cures are best for olives picked green; the lye draws out the bitterness, and the salt in the brine draws out moisture and adds flavor. Fully ripe black olives are less bitter and don't need a lye treatment. Unless very small, they are usually salt cured dry. (Big ones get too soft if cured in brine.)

Here is a recipe for brine-cured green olives: Soak 3 gallons of unbruised green olives in a gallon of water with 3 tablespoons lye. After 24 hours, drain the olives and rinse until clear. Then soak them for 48 hours in a gallon of water with 4 tablespoons lye. Drain and rinse again, and put them to soak a third time in a gallon of water with 2 tablespoons salt. After 24 hours, drain and rinse and put the olives to soak a fourth time in a gallon of water with 4 tablespoons salt. After 48 hours, rinse the olives and let them sit for two weeks in brine of the same strength (1 quart water for 1 tablespoon salt). Every 2 weeks, change the brine. Refrigerated, the olives will keep several months.

Here are some types of olives we use. Picholine olives are small French olives – green, brine cured, crisp, and a bit tart. Tiny black Niçoise olives are picked ripe, brine cured, and packed in oil; they have a distinctive smoky flavor. Nyons olives are also from Provence; they are small, round, reddish brown, and pleasantly bitter. Olives from the town of Gaeta near Naples are small and smooth, picked ripe and black, and brine cured; they taste very ripe. Greek Kalamata olives are picked red- or purple-ripe and cured for 2 weeks in salt brine; vinegar is added to them when they're packed.

Store brine-cured olives in their own brine. Keep salt-cured olives in the refrigerator, packed in layers of salt or in olive oil.

Olive paste, a purée of ripe black olives and olive oil, is imported from Italy and sold at some fancy grocery stores. The best products are unseasoned and unadulterated.

179

Olive oil is an indispensable ingredient. The best is first pressing, cold-pressed, unfiltered extra virgin. Olives grown specifically for oil are harvested as they begin to ripen in the winter, ground into a paste, pressed, and centrifuged to separate the oil from the other liquids and wastes. (The paste pressed again with heat yields a second pressing oil.) The oil must have less than 1% acidity to be classified as extra virgin.

Real olive oil varies from year to year, just like wine. Even in the same year the first olive oil made from less ripe olives will be greener, more highly flavored, and contain more residue than later on. Imported real olive oil is expensive, unfortunately. No California olive oil compares in quality to the better Tuscan and French oils.

Heat compromises the flavor and nutritional value of very good olive oil. For frying at high temperatures or just for a lighter, less rich taste, you may need a lighter olive oil. Oil can also be perfumed with basil leaves, marjoram, or red pepper.

Pancetta is a peppery, tasty Italian kind of salt pork. Lean pork belly is salted for about 2 weeks, rinsed, seasoned with pepper and spices, rolled into a neat cylinder, wrapped in a thin casing, aged, and then sliced thin. Unlike American bacon, it is dry cured and not smoked at all.

Parmesan is the most famous of the *grana* cheeses (the generic Italian name for hard, grainy cheeses). The only real Parmesan is Parmigiano Reggiano from Parma, Italy. When the cheese is aged many years, its flavor improves and its price increases; the relatively young moist kind is not perfect for grating, but it is wonderful served with a little virgin olive oil and some good bread.

Pepper in this book means whole black peppercorns ground fresh. Peppercorns are the berries of the pepper plant (*Piper nigrum*). They are picked green, freeze-dried or canned, and sold as green peppercorns; picked unripe and dried (these are black peppercorns); or picked ripe, hulled, and dried (white peppercorns).

Red or pink peppercorns, however, are the dried berries of either of two New World plants unrelated to the Old World pepper plant: the Peruvian or California pepper tree (*Schinus molle*) or the Brazilian pepper tree (*Schinus terebinthifolius*). They can be found on the shelves of some fancy grocery stores.

Peppers, roasted and peeled, are used in several recipes. To do this, cook the peppers on the grill, over the gas flame of the stove, or in the hottest part of the oven until the skin turns black and will peel off. Let them cool, then peel away the charred skin and remove the seeds and stem. Use the back of a paring knife to scrape off the remaining little bits of black or wipe clean with a towel. Then, depending on their intended use, cut into wide strips and marinate in a garlic-basil vinaigrette, or cut into fine julienne, or chop, or purée . . .

Prosciutto is a dry-cured, aged ham. For any ham, variables affecting quality include the type of pig, its diet, and the way it was butchered; the sort of cure it received (dry salted or brine cured); and the length and method of aging. Italian prosciutto must conform to stringent controls: the pigs must be butchered and bled in certain ways (different hams have different shapes according to the permitted butchering method), aging must last at least 9 months, and so forth. We cannot get genuine Italian prosciutto (federal law prohibits importing uncooked pork products), but Italian butchers in this country make reasonable facsimiles.

The best domestic prosciutto is made from pigs with firm muscle and fat. The hams are salted, rinsed, and dried; rubbed with pepper, herbs, and spices; pressed; hung to age for several months; and rubbed with olive oil and pepper from time to time.

Most places that sell prosciutto will also sell you the prosciutto bone, which can be used to flavor soups, stews, sauces, beans, and so forth.

Quail eggs can be bought from some poulterers and fancy grocery stores. Their higher proportion of yolk to white makes them very tasty, and their size makes them an appealing garnish for certain dishes, like the salad on page 108.

Radicchio is the Italian name for any of several varieties of red chicory. Some form compact roundish hearts, others have longer loose leaves and tapered hearts. The leaves are a beautiful deep red with white ribs, or streaked and variegated red, white, and green. They have a very crunchy texture and a pleasantly bitter taste.

Originally a winter salad, radicchio is now available almost year round from Italy and elsewhere in Europe. Already successful at growing the Belgian endive, another kind of chicory, Belgian farmers are starting to produce radicchio on a large scale. Imported radicchio is expensive, but enterprising American growers are experimenting with its cultivation.

Ricotta is a soft white cottage cheese made from both cow's and sheep's milk. It is rather bland and sweet with a moist, crumbly texture. There is also an Italian version called ricotta pecorino that is dry and salty. In many parts of the country it should be possible to find a fresh ricotta, locally made by small producers.

Romano is a very hard, dry, salty, and tangy sheep's milk cheese usually grated and used on gratins and pasta. There is a considerable difference between Italian and domestic versions. Of the many Italian varieties, pepato is noteworthy; it is aged with black peppercorns in the center and is excellent for pasta.

Shrimp and prawns used for recipes in this book may be any fresh local variety. (Nomenclature is confused: in California, "prawns" is generally used to describe large shrimp.) To peel shrimp or prawns, first wash them in cold water and remove their heads. Holding the shrimp by its tail with one hand, peel off the top half of the shell with the other, then squeeze the base of the tail and the shrimp will slip out of the remaining shell.

Grass shrimp are tiny shrimp (150 to the pound) found on the Pacific Coast. They are like the tiny Atlantic shrimp known in France as *crevettes grises*. When raw they are translucent. When cooked they turn gray with a hint of pink. They are delicate and are generally eaten in the shell, which has a great flavor and a crunchy texture when fried.

Squid from both the Pacific and the Atlantic are easy to clean. Cut off the tentacles just above the eyes. Squeeze out and discard the hard little beak inside the tentacles at the point where they join the head. Use your fingers to pull out the guts and the cuttlebone, or quill, from the body. Rinse in cold water and drain. If the squid is to be cut in strips instead of in rings, you can slit the bodies up one side, spread them flat, and scrape clean with the back of a knife. Small squid are best cooked hot and fast for maximum tenderness. Cooked too slowly or for too long they soon turn tough. Large squid, on the other hand, stay tough unless stewed a little.

Stocks are fundamental to many recipes and essential to fine sauces.

Chicken Stock

2 carrots
1 large onion
1 or 2 leeks
2 stalks celery
¼ pound fresh mushrooms
1 whole chicken

3 to 4 quarts water
A few cloves garlic
2 bay leaves
2 or 3 sprigs fresh thyme
Several sprigs fresh parsley
Salt

Peel the carrots and onion. Trim the leeks, cut in half, and rinse well. Slice all of the vegetables and mushrooms and put them in a pot with the chicken and water. Bring the water to a boil, reduce to a simmer, and skim thoroughly during the first 15 minutes. The protein matter suspended in the water solidifies when the water boils, and floats to the top. This foamy substance and the fat must be removed if the stock is to be clear and without off-flavors. After this first skimming, add the herbs and a little salt. Simmer the stock for 3 to 4 hours, skimming occasionally. If the stock is allowed to boil with the fat still in the liquid, the two will emulsify and the broth will be hopelessly cloudy. Long cooking at a whisper of a simmer and attentive skimming will result in a stock of fine clarity and flavor. Strain and remove any fat from the surface. Use as is for a light broth or reduce it for a more concentrated flavor.

Beef Stock

Because of the proportions of meat and bone, beef shank makes excellent stock. Brown the meat in a roasting pan in the oven. The browning will give color and roasted flavor to the broth and will render some of the fat and blood from the meat. Proceed as if making chicken stock with the usual complement of aromatic vegetables. Add some tomatoes and mushrooms. Start with plenty of water; during the long cooking (about twice as long as chicken stock), quite a bit will be lost to evaporation. Again we emphasize the importance of thorough skimming and slow cooking.

Squab or Duck Stock

It is expensive to use whole pigeons or duck just for stock. If you are roasting the birds, the carcasses alone will make very good stock, especially if you use chicken stock instead of water to moisten the bones and vegetables. If you have boned pigeon or duck for some other purposes and have uncooked carcasses remaining, brown them in the oven and use them for the base of a good broth. Use all the trimmed parts of the birds as well: head, neck, feet, and wing tips. Proceed as if making chicken stock. The addition of fresh tomato, mushrooms, and shallots will enrich the flavor.

Fish Stock or Fumet

2 fish skeletons	3 or 4 shallots
1 fish head	6 or 7 ripe tomatoes
6 clams	2 cloves garlic
6 mussels	½ to ⅓ bottle white wine
2 or 3 carrots	Black pepper
1 large onion	Orange peel (1 or 2 strips)
2 leeks	2 or 3 sprigs each: parsley, basil,
1 stalk celery	thyme, bay leaf, fennel

Clean the fish carcasses very well. Remove the gills and all bloody parts, as they impart a bitter and unpleasant taste. Scrub the clams and mussels. Peel and clean all the aromatic vegetables and roughly chop or slice them. Chop the tomatoes. Put everything together in a stock pot, including the herbs, seasoning, and white wine. Cover with 3 or 4 quarts of water and bring to a boil. Lower the heat to a simmer and skim very thoroughly during the first 15 minutes. Cook for approximately 1½ hours. Skim occasionally. Strain and taste. Reduce the stock if a very robust flavor is wanted, or use as is. Any number of combinations of fish and shellfish will make wonderful broth. It just depends on what is available, and how you plan to use the broth.

Sun-dried tomatoes, imported from Italy, have an intense flavor – piquant, salty, and a little spicy. The home-cured ones that we have tasted are milder and sweeter. Here is a method to make your own.

Choose ripe full-flavored tomatoes that are on the firm side. Plum tomatoes or other varieties that have a lot of flesh in proportion to juice will work best. Yellow pear-shaped cherry tomatoes taste wonderful dried. Cut the tomatoes in half lengthwise and squeeze out the seeds and excess juice. Set them so that they are not touching one another on a screen or tray that allows some air to circulate around them. Salt lightly with fine sea salt, which will help to extract moisture and inhibit the growth of bacteria. Cover the tomatoes (without actually touching them) with a piece of cheesecloth, to keep out insects. Set them out in the sun during the day and take them in at night. How long it takes to dry them depends on weather conditions, probably between 3 and 5 days. When they have dried, pack them tightly in sterilized jars and cover with olive oil. Press the layers to squeeze out any air bubbles and seal the jar. You may wish to flavor some with basil leaves or cayenne pepper.

Tomatoes can be quickly peeled and seeded. Immerse tomatoes, a few at a time, in boiling water for 10 to 20 seconds (the riper they are, the less time they will take). Remove and plunge them immediately into cold water. Use a paring knife to remove the core and slip or peel off the skin. Cut the tomatoes in half crosswise and dislodge the seeds with your fingertips or squeeze the tomato halves and shake loose the seeds.

When we refer to tomatoes in this book, we mean vine-ripened tomatoes in season.

Truffles are wild edible fungi that produce their fruiting bodies underground. There are numerous European and American species, but only two are widely commercialized: the white truffle found only in Italy, and the black truffle found in the Périgord region of France, and in parts of Italy, Spain, and Germany.

Once acquired, a taste for truffles is difficult to lose, despite their high price. Their arrival becomes a very special seasonal event. White truffles are the first to appear in the fall. More perishable than black truffles, white ones should be eaten raw, sliced very thin over something hot. Their complex, penetrating odor is best appreciated when their taste is foremost in a dish. Black truffles, on the other hand, which come into season in December, are enhanced by cooking. Black truffles sliced and baked with a potato gratin, incorporated into a stuffing, or cooked in a lobster soup can enrich and transform a meal.

Buy truffles only if they are fresh, aromatic, firm, and free of holes. If they are soft, or if they smell the least bit ammoniated, they're not worth the trouble or expense. Store them buried in dry rice or individually wrapped in a sealed container. Eat them soon.

Wild mushrooms have recently become more available: fresh chanterelles, oyster mushrooms, boletes, and others are now sold in specialty markets, in season. Hunting and gathering wild mushrooms is possible even in the urban environment in parks and woodlands. There are many good books on the subject. We recommend David Arora's *Mushrooms Demystified* (Berkeley: Ten Speed Press, 1979). For the beginner we suggest that you confirm the exact species of your finds with an expert. Many communities have mycological societies, colleges, or universities where this can be done. The mushrooms mentioned in this book are:

Chanterelles (*Cantharellus cibarius*)
Wood blewits (*Tricholoma nudum*)
Field mushrooms (*Agaricus campestris*)
Shaggy parasol (*Lepiota rhacodes*)
Morel (*Morchella esculenta*)
Boletus, porcini, cèpe (*Boletus edulis*)
Horn of plenty (*Craterellus cornucopioides*)
Oyster mushroom (*Pleurotus ostreatus*)
Hedgehog mushroom (*Dentinum repandum*)

Index

About the Authors

ALICE WATERS left Chatham, New Jersey, for Berkeley, California, where she opened Chez Panisse in 1971. In 1980 she opened a café on the floor above Chez Panisse, with an à la carte menu featuring pasta, pizza, and calzone. In 1982 Alice Waters wrote the *Chez Panisse Menu Cookbook*, and she is currently working on the *Chez Panisse Dessert Cookbook* with Lindsey Shere, the pastry chef at Chez Panisse. *Chez Panisse Pasta, Pizza, & Calzone* was written in collaboration with Patricia Curtan and Martine Labro.

PATRICIA CURTAN, a native Californian, has cooked with Alice Waters since 1979 at Chez Panisse while continuing to work as a professional printer and designer. She transcribed and organized the recipes and designed *Chez Panisse Pasta, Pizza, & Calzone*.

MARTINE LABRO, an artist and designer, was born in France and lives and cooks in Provence. She contributed her favorite Provençal recipes and did all the drawings for *Chez Panisse Pasta, Pizza, & Calzone*.